Luigi's

Jazz
Warm
Up

Luigi's

Jazz Warm Up

And Introduction To Jazz Style & Technique

Luigi
Jazz Dance Innovator

Lorraine Person Kriegel, M.A.
Dancer/Choreographer

Francis James Roach
Teacher/Choreographer

A Dance Horizons Book
Princeton Book Company, Publishers
Pennington, New Jersey
1997

A Dance Horizons Book
Princeton Book Company, Publishers
P.O. Box 57
Pennington, New Jersey 08534

The models for the Luigi exercises are Lucia Tristan and Luigi.

Interior book design by Lorraine Person Kriegel.

Printed in Canada

Library of Congress Cataloging-in-Publication Data

Luigi.
        Luigi's jazz warm up : and introduction to jazz style and technique
/ Luigi, Lorraine Kriegel, Francis Roach ; with photographs by Lee Kraft.
        p.   cm.
    ISBN 0-87127-202-4
    1. Jazz dance.   I. Kriegel, Lorraine Person. II. Roach, Francis,
1956-   . III. Title
GV1784.L85 . 1997
781-65'09--dc20   97-32734
                                                                    CIP

I dedicate this book to all the dancers and teachers carrying on the Luigi Technique. My special thanks to my co-authors for reminding me to remember.

Many thanks and never stop moving.

Love, Luigi

For Gary, my partner in the Dance.

LPK

For Luigi

FJR

TABLE OF CONTENTS

INTRODUCTION

When I teach, I feel first and then I say.
If I like it, I give it.
If I don't like it, I don't give it.
I only give what I like.
I call it "feeling from the inside."

To exercise, find the right feeling and the right
sound inside you.

To dance, put your hand on your heart and
listen to the sound of your soul.

Art

When I dance I'm telling you about myself. Every exercise of my technique is the story of my life. I don't want my students to dance like I do, I don't want them to dance what I feel—my feeling is my feeling. I want them to dance their feeling. As a teacher, that's my goal: to get to the feeling inside.

As you do these exercises, don't think of what you have done in class before or what you will be doing six months from now; think only in the now. Dance what you are right now.

Part of moving from the inside means that you dance within the limits of your own body and you do only what you feel. Never force anything. Never lose control; nothing should hurt. Technique is like tuning an instrument. Learn to tune your body just right, so that when you go to play it, it's beautiful. *The beauty of dancing is the control of it.*

I became a teacher in order to share with you what I learned from my own rehabilitation and to give you my lifelong experiences in show business. In my technique you learn how to be a professional from the beginning.

Learn to develop your technique by knowing what you are doing, rather than pretending or imitating. *You must know your body in order to feel the movement in all directions.* In every position feel the muscles and the blood flowing through the body by putting the body into the right position.

Begin slowly, and feel everything you are doing from the inside. As you learn to put the body in the right place, you will discover new sensations and enjoy the feeling of every part of the body working together—*feeling from the inside.*

Always try to find the inside control rather than the outside, wasted energy. Try to find everything you are doing from the inside, and constantly make adjustments to feel the body in the right position. In that way you will develop control and heal your own body. *A true warm up done right will give you strength—not wear you out.*

Before you start any exercise, put the body in balance, using every part of the body—never isolating one part. *It takes the whole body to make a good standing position or any position.* In order to exercise right, the posture and body position must first be correct. Learn to control and protect the body at the same time. Use everything inside the body to get through to the outside.

I believe that exercises, when not done right, are wrong for the body. The important things to know about controlling and protecting the body are the proper placements. These are the parts of the body that I have to use to find strong placements:

1. Always pull in the stomach and use the abdominal muscles, lifting up underneath the rib cage to strengthen the back.

2. Pull the shoulders down, using the armpits, and stretch the muscles in the back up to lift the upper part of the body.

3. Tighten the buttocks to pull up on the thighs and build the muscles up around the knees.

I say, use the correct placements for your body to be better, and keep repeating them until they become a good habit and second nature. Pull the shoulders down, suck in the stomach and squeeze the buttocks. Use them with some of the general tips I give to everyone.

- Always keep the upper part of the body lifted away from the lower part.
- Use the stomach muscles so as not to arch the back.
- Press the pelvis forward and stay above it.
- Always keep the knees over the toes.
- Guide your arms from the back and stretch the muscles "open across your back."
- Focus front. Always look where you are going.
- Never force the body into a position.
- Make adjustments; constantly make adjustments to find the control and the feeling.
- NEVER STOP MOVING.

When teaching the use of the arms, I emphasize using the *whole* body. Don't use your arms from your shoulder; use your arms from the back. Feel the muscles lengthening from across the back all the way into the fingertips, as if you have one long arm across the back. Stretching the muscles out keeps you from overdeveloping and tensing the muscles across the back. Mostly, it gives you better alignment and balance. Try not to pull or pinch the shoulders back whenever you stand or do anything. Use the back, use the armpits, and open across the back. Also, keep the shoulders down and the elbows curved, so that there's a professional look. By pressing the arms out and into the space around you, you learn to *feel the space*. Use the space around you to support yourself and keep your balance. *Whenever you need support, you do it yourself.*

Whether I'm teaching a beginner or a professional, I say to them: "You're bound to make a slight mistake once in awhile. But when you make that little mistake, make an adjustment. That adjustment could become a beautiful sound." Your arms are bound to lift a little sometimes, or drop a little sometimes, but keep making adjustments. Adjustments become the phrasing of the body. Besides, there should be variations of the body so that if it goes out of line for a second, you automatically put it back into place—shading a movement beautifully.

The <u>most</u> important advice I can give you is:

LEARN HOW TO LEARN. Learn by getting through to the feeling inside. Do this by keeping your mind on "now," this moment and every moment. Constantly be aware of what you are feeling and what you are doing to get that feeling. What feels the best is the best thing to do. Especially when repeating something, always find something new and different and make it better. Let it grow, let it develop without getting tired of it. Regardless of whether you are a teacher, dancer, singer, actor, or in some other profession:

- Take every class as though it were your first class.
- Do each exercise as if it were a whole class.
- Learn about the body, about your feelings, about getting better, about life.

In this way you will constantly develop yourself and keep your mind open for learning.

Luigi

Facts

After twenty years of acrobatics, singing, and dancing experience as a child entertainer, Luigi woke up one day in a hospital bed, unable to move. "You're paralyzed; you'll never walk again," his doctor said.

He had been on his way to buy ballet shoes when the driver of the car he was in lost control on a rainy Hollywood street. Luigi was thrown from the car and his head was crushed against the curb. He almost died on the street, then went into a coma that lasted for many days. The left side of his face and the right side of his body were paralyzed. He had a fractured skull and a broken jaw. He was unable to control the muscles in his eyes because they were jarred and stretched. The doctors held out little hope that Luigi would recover, and no hope he that he would walk again. But Luigi knew he would dance again, because a voice inside was talking to him. *Never stop moving, kid. If you stop moving, you're dead. Don't ever stop moving.* Luigi has never lost touch with that voice.

Luigi's desire to dance again left him no alternative but to create his own ideas of learning to move the body correctly—all the time. He discovered, the hard way, that movement must come totally from the inside out. From that day to this, Luigi has embodied that direct "feeling from the inside" approach of balance and control to every position of his body. In his teaching, not only does he explain the "why and wherefore" of jazz dance movements, but he consistently points out the need to understand the proper positions for ballet, tap, modern, acrobatics, singing, and acting. He even includes daily events such as sleeping and "waiting for the light to change" standing positions.

His lifted torso, strong épaulements and hips always in alignment—all are purely classical ballet. The natural plié, his "close-lock fourth," and never forcing or holding a position are American jazz.

Born in 1925, Eugene Facciuto grew up in a large Italian-American family in Steubenville, Ohio. (Much later, he was nicknamed "Luigi" by his friend, the dancer and choreographer Gene Kelly.) Luigi's flexibility and "putting things in their right place" started early when he was still a child acrobat. The superb timing of movements, however, came from his experience as a young tap dancer and teenage Big Band singer in America's heartland during the 1930's and '40s. Certainly all those elements—plus his accident and rehabilitation—contributed to what was to become the world's first complete jazz dance technique. With overwhelming success and the encouragement of others, in 1949, he began sharing the "Luigi Style."

It was in 1946 that this 21-year-old G.I., home unscathed from World War II, awoke from a coma to be told: "You'll never walk again." But his inner voice took over, and it kept saying, "Never stop moving, kid." His spirit of determination told him, "You're gonna dance again." After months of conventional therapy, Luigi came to understand that what he was doing by himself was regaining control and strength faster than anyone expected. Thus, he started his own intense questioning of his body, which, in answer, became a routine warm up. Miraculously, within a year, he was walking back into dance classes looking for help and pushing his body to rid itself of the paralysis, just as he still does today.

Luigi has studied with some of the world's renowned performers and choreographers, all of whom became teachers. Adolph Bolm, Bronislava Nijinska, Michel Panaieff, and Edward Caton, who instilled in him a love of the Cecchetti ballet method. Eugene Loring and Sally Whalen taught Luigi the Fokine ballet approach. Louis Da Pron helped confirm his early training in the "crystal clear, light on your feet" tap style, as did Miss Edith Jane. This special lady took Luigi on as her protégé at Falcon Studios, opening her arms as well as the musical theater and film world to this young Italian-American. Because she danced with Michel Fokine, her ballet and character dance were also excellent training. Famous circus acrobatic teacher Sam Mintz, Olympic fencing gold medalist Ralph Faulkner, and dancer/choreographer Michio Ito all taught at Falcon Studios and left an artistic mark on Luigi. His determination to dance again was fueled by working with these great artists.

Two years after Luigi's accident, a Metro-Goldwyn-Mayer Film Studio talent scout spotted him in a Falcon Studios recital. He was brought to Gene Kelly who hired him for the musical, "On the Town." Amazingly, Luigi was working the paralyzed side of his body so well that he began an eight-year career as a chorus dancer in such films as "Annie Get Your Gun," "An American in Paris," "Singin' in the Rain," "The Band Wagon," and "White Christmas," to name a few. Choreographers Robert Alton, Hermes Pan, Eugene Loring, and Michael Kidd used him with stars Fred Astaire, Cyd Charisse, Judy Garland, Leslie Caron, Bing Crosby, Donald O'Connor, Vera Ellen, and Danny Kaye. Luigi is proudest of being known as an "MGM, Gene Kelly, and Bob Alton boy" in the golden era of Hollywood musicals.

During the rehearsals on film sets he continued to do his own expanded warm up for balance and flexibility, and soon dancers were following him, ten or twenty at a time. With more encouragement, he started teaching open classes in his "classical jazz" in 1951 at Rainbow Studios in Hollywood. Also, he was asked to form many nightclub acts for himself and others, using his style. In addition to earning extra money, this gave Luigi an opportunity to showcase his own choreography, which brought such stars as Joan Crawford and Rita Hayworth backstage to compliment his work and dancing. Luigi continued to teach even as he performed in nightclubs, movies, and early live television productions in Los Angeles. He never stopped moving.

Near the end of 1956, Luigi was brought to New York City to perform with Ethel Merman and Fernando Lamas in their Broadway show, "Happy Hunting." It was at this time that June Taylor asked him to teach at her famous dance school. After being there awhile he formed his own independent classes again. Into the early

1960's, he continued to perform and assist choreographers Alex Romero, Lee Scott, and Onna White, for a total of four Broadway shows. Yet Luigi, who loved teaching, felt he had something to share artistically and dedicated himself to forming a school. Today he teaches two, sometimes three or four, classes a day at Luigi's Jazz Centre in New York City.

Luigi's roster of famous students is legendary. In Los Angeles there were Francois Szony, Ken Berry, Barrie Chase, Sheree North, Johnny Brascia, Jillanna and Jacques D'Amboise. In New York, he taught Alvin Ailey, Michael Bennett, Sheila Bond, Kevin Carlisle, Yvonne Constance, Peggy Fleming, Valerie Harper, Madonna, Patricia McBride, Donna McKechnie, Liza Minnelli, Robert Morse, Ann Reinking, Susan Stroman, Hama, Rhett Dennis, Twyla Tharp, John Travolta, Iva Withers and Gretchen Wyler and Christopher Walken.

Luigi has taught master classes throughout North and South America, in Germany, France, England, Hungary, South Africa, and Japan. He has served on the faculties of the Harkness Ballet School, the High School of Performing Arts, Kingsborough Community College, New York University, and the Metropolitan Opera House. For five years, Luigi had his own jazz dance company, which performed internationally. His technique is taught today by students and their students in schools and colleges all over the world.

Clearly, his dancing is part of what makes Luigi an innovator. He has the heart, love, and ambition to redesign, to "break new ground," to create a style that brings the best of dancing forward and establishes a strong foundation for future generations. Luigi is indeed a pioneer and an artist.

When asked his definition of an artist, Luigi simply says, *An artist is first a human being. One who gives of himself unselfishly. One who leaves something behind.*

Francis James Roach

Theory

I had just finished interviewing Susan Stroman, a successful Broadway choreographer. As she was showing me to the door, I asked one last question: "Before you choreograph or before you go into a rehearsal, do you warm up?" She immediately reached her right arm up and then her left, as if starting a Luigi class. "Of course," she said, "we all have those Luigi exercises in our bodies, in our blood. We don't even have to think about it anymore."

It seems every dancer knows Luigi or knows of him. He created the first comprehensive jazz dance technique, and it has since spread around the world. Even young dancers who don't know the name know the exercises because they are the exercises that have come to define the art of jazz dance. They are the "gold standard" of jazz dance technique.

When asked why his technique is so popular, Luigi is quick to answer:

> *It's the rhythm of the body and the feeling with which you get there.*

He repeats this complex phrase in most classes and on his records, CD's and videotapes. If many students don't understand intellectually what he means, they certainly understand and *feel* his meaning when they start to dance.

> *When dancing, you must not intellectualize. Forget about yourself. For right now you are not you—you are tuning up your body to become sound.*

It is the nature of dance technique to transcend language, so any attempt to explain dance will fall short but, for several reasons, it is worthwhile to try and capture the technique in pictures and words. For one, there are many of Luigi's students and his students' students teaching his technique in colleges and universities as well as in academies and in studios. This book will help them by serving as a basis for theoretical analysis and as a supplemental text to class. Secondly, over the years Luigi's dance has spread far from the source, making a codified set of principles helpful in preserving the fundamentals. Lastly, Luigi's technique has now become so evolved, so honed and widespread as a system of dance training, that its principles are almost within the reach of the intellect—much as are those of classical ballet. Almost within the intellect's reach, but, as Luigi understands so well, words can't do it justice:

> *It's the sound, the sound, the sound. I dance the sound.*

In this book, Part One introduces some important elements of the technique. Part Two includes 434 photographs of the exercises, with precise instructions on how you should feel as you do them. Whenever possible, the authors have used Luigi's expressions, words and phrases to communicate the feeling of the dance. Sometimes we have sacrificed English syntax for "dance syntax." There may be some sentences that seem to go on too long, or words that seem unfamiliar or counterintuitive. We recommend that you dance the phrases—try them on your body. We've often let words flow one into the other because the movements do. Unfamiliar terms, such as "stretch-point," or verbs used as nouns, such as "side-stretch right," will make sense in the context of the instructions if you let them dance for you.

This book will be especially valuable for the beginning dancer who wants to learn to dance properly from the start. As Luigi says:

> *If you keep doing things right long enough, they'll get better, right. But if you keep doing things wrong long enough, they'll feel right, wrong.*

Some concepts may seem difficult at first, but the important ones are repeated often as we proceed through the warm up. Repetition is an important part of training. Nothing in the warm up is too difficult for a beginner, because in this technique the dancer is always in control of the movements, working within his or her capability. Nevertheless, there is a lifetime's worth of material here that will take time and practice to understand and master.

More advanced dancers and teachers of the Luigi style and other jazz dance styles will find the book an invaluable reference and a reminder of the basic principles of safe technique.

Perhaps the most exciting aspect of studying with Luigi is the diversity of students at his school. Luigi students come in all shapes and sizes and in every state of physical and mental development. Actors, singers, children, senior citizens, stroke victims, accident survivors, dancers and writers are united in his class, going through the same exercises at whatever level of physical and mental understanding they can summon. Luigi is much more than a dance teacher, as you will discover in the pages of this book.

There is also a special audience Luigi hopes to reach—dancers and non-dancers with physical disabilities. Luigi has lived through the experience of rehabilitation and muscular reprogramming. He is an inspiring guide to the physical achievements that are possible against seemingly impossible odds. His story is an example of overcoming physical and mental adversity, one that offers hope to those facing a similar struggle.

Lorraine Person Kriegel

Friends

This book has been a labor of love—Luigi's love for his art and his students; and a labor of respect—our respect for the life and genius of Luigi. The authors are proud that we have put the definitive analysis of Luigi's warm up on record. We have tried to make it clear and detailed so that the technique will live on for centuries after us. This is no exaggeration: Luigi's jazz technique has already spread around the world and will continue, like ballet, as another cohesive language of dance.

The book was a tremendously complex undertaking and could not have been finished without the help of a great many dance lovers, foremost among them the very encouraging Charles Woodford of Princeton Book Company and copyeditor Roy Grisham.

Thanks, too, to the band at Power Color in New York, who made digital music in assembling the book, including Anthony Ramos and Bob Carmelitano on Prismax; Tim Grey and Al Simpson on high-resolution scanner; Dalila Hachani and Ted Goldberg on Macintosh; Camilla Marstrand for her cover design; Rich Loffredo, the leader of the band; and Hubert Kriegel, impresario.

Thanks to Jeff and Annette Miller and to Mitch Daniels for their help; and to Charles Salzberg, Sarah Slagle, Julia James for reviewing parts of the manuscript. John Boyd was encouraging and helpful at the most crucial time with design suggestions and encouragement. Special thanks goes to Dr. Arthur Iberall for being a rigorous and graceful intellectual example and to Maurice LaPue, dancer and loyal friend of dancers.

Luigi thanks the Facciuto family for their love and support.

Part One

FOUNDATION OF THE TECHNIQUE

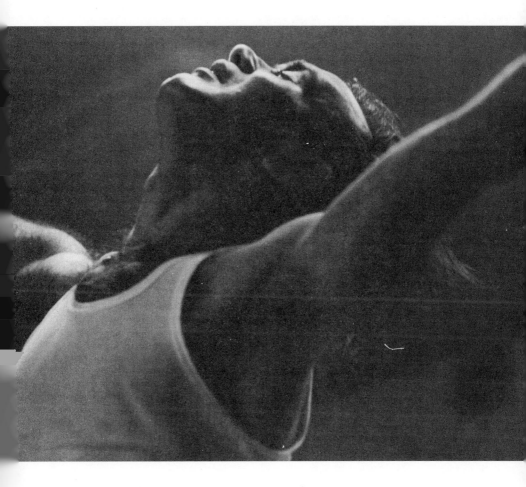

Your Space Is Your Barre

One of the foundations of my technique is, *your space is your barre*. After my accident, I learned to use my whole body by finding the right position for every movement I made. I learned where the muscles begin and where they end. Starting from scratch gave me the chance to do everything right from the beginning. I had to find what muscles I used to control the body while standing at the dance barre and how to find that same inner feeling away from the barre.

I teach that when you are away from the barre, feel that an imaginary barre is always there for support. This develops control, helping you to feel the arms pressing down against the space around you for balance, and teaches you not to throw the arms out of line. This also gives you awareness of the natural arm alignment used in dance, called second position: the curved elbow below the pulled-down shoulder, the wrist below the elbow and the fingertips below the wrist, as if correctly placed on a ballet barre.

Whenever you need help balancing, do it yourself.

Luigi

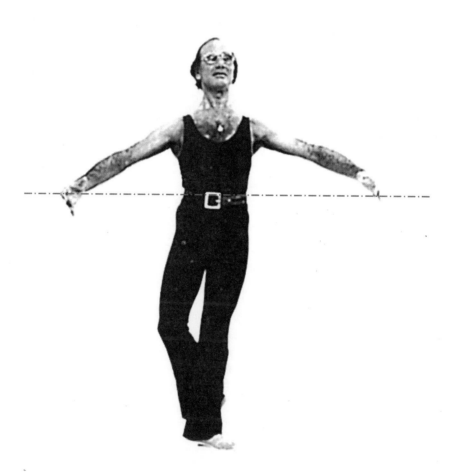

Principles of the Technique

The Luigi Warm Up is a system of dance exercises that prepare a dancer physically, intellectually, and spiritually to dance. It is a system that has evolved and been refined over the years into a dance technique that has become the universal standard—the *lingua franca*—of jazz dance.

The warm-up exercises documented in this book, if done correctly, will stretch, strengthen, and integrate body and mind at a profound level. The exercises work quickly, efficiently, and safely. To understand why they work as well as they do, it is important to understand how and why they were developed.

It is no exaggeration to say that Luigi's journey to international fame was a heroic one—heroic in the mythological sense Joseph Campbell describes in his famous book, *The Hero with a Thousand Faces*. The heroic journey is a solitary ordeal, with many challenges to be overcome. By overcoming them, Campbell's mythological hero eventually achieves a new level of understanding and brings his knowledge back to the village or tribe. Luigi, indeed, went on a solitary journey. For five or six years of rehabilitation after a nearly fatal car accident, he endured pain and discouragement; but he learned something important and new about the body, and ever since, he has been sharing this knowledge with the world: how to heal the body, how to make it strong, how to free it to dance, and how to teach it to live.

I learned to love before I learned how to dance.

There is a lot of love in the Luigi technique, and thousands of students in our tribe of gypsy dancers in our global village have greatly benefited from Luigi's enlightened level of understanding.

As with any journey, the hard part is to start. After his accident, Luigi was wheeled into a dance studio, where he fell over and over again. He got so much blood on the floor, the owner threatened to ban him. Eventually, though, Luigi became strong enough to stand—then, with the help of the ballet barre, to move.

It was learning to stand *without* the barre—using an imaginary barre—that became the first principle of the Luigi technique. He pretended to have a barre when he needed it. By pressing on that imaginary barre in space, Luigi found his balance and learned what adjustments to make in order to maintain his equilibrium. That was the first step in making his body beautiful again.

> *During the years following my accident, I was learning where the muscles begin and where the muscles end. I wasn't concentrating on any one muscle or body part; I was learning to control the whole body. I didn't want people to see my injured face. I wanted people to watch my body, so I did things to make my body look beautiful.*

In what we would today call a neuromuscular visualization exercise, Luigi isometrically stabilized his body by imagining the help of a ballet barre. Here's how he describes it:

> *I feel the space around me. If you think you need the support of a barre, a cane, or a crutch, lift up and feel the space around you instead. Realize that you can support yourself by using that space and by using your body as a whole, not by isolating its parts or dividing it into left and right sides.*

It's important to remember that Luigi wasn't a beginner when he began developing his technique. He was a professional dancer with a disabled body. He'd had solid training in classical ballet and had great respect for the technique. He had also studied eurhythmics and modern dance with Michio Ito, in addition to acrobatics and tap dancing. Thus, with a sophisticated understanding of dance training but a completely uncooperative body, Luigi set about retraining himself to dance.

In order to do that, he had to *feel from the inside*, the second important principle of the Luigi Technique. From his solid base, Luigi learned to move in all directions of dance—front, side, back, and diagonal; and it all came from one place—the inside.

> *I try to feel the inside control, to feel everything moving into place, to feel the body breathing and to feel it never stop moving. I'm aware of the sensation of lifting up the top of the body in order to free the bottom to move without injury, of lengthening the spine to protect it from a slipped disc or a pinched nerve, of using my arms from all the way across my back and not just the shoulders. I feel my stomach lifted up underneath my rib cage and pulled in to protect my back. I feel the buttocks tightening to strengthen my legs and pelvis. I'm aware of not straining the backs of the legs, so that I protect my knees from injury.*

Feeling from the Inside

Luigi's warm-up exercises, when experienced in class, are quiet and controlled; they are almost meditative. Luigi doesn't exhort, push, or cheerlead. Instead, he allows the dancers to *feel from the inside*.

Every dancer in Luigi's class is different—a different individual, a different dancer—and all of them are at different levels of physical and mental understanding of the technique. Luigi gives each the space to discover the dancer within. He provides encouragement, safety, and an inspiring example as he leads his exercises. His students progress at a remarkable rate by *feeling from the inside*.

What does this phrase mean? *Feeling from the inside* is putting the body in the right place, where it feels good and safe, and *feeling* as it moves to the next position. Like the technique itself, feeling from the inside is a concept that works on different levels, meaning something different for the beginner than for the advanced dancer.

For the beginner, dancing from the inside may mean paying attention to how the body feels as it goes through the movements. It can be difficult for the beginner in most dance classes. You are bombarded with new experiences: the music is blaring, the teacher is demonstrating, the movements are unfamiliar, the other students all seem to know more than you, and you're not very comfortable wearing tights. Luigi says:

> *Feel from the inside. Don't be distracted by externals. Focus on your body. Don't do anything that hurts. Don't pretend. Don't do anything faster than you want. Watch it, feel it, and then move.*

For the intermediate dancer, feeling from the inside may involve integrating and harmonizing each movement so that it moves and flows. Luigi does not believe in isolating, neither movements nor body parts. He believes in integration.

> *Dance isn't about isolating. It's about using everything inside of you to make a sound. I don't separate the body; I keep the body connected.*

> *I have always used the good to make the weak stronger. The right side helps the left side, the upper torso helps the lower torso. The body works together as a whole.*

> *Isolation is not a good word. It implies cutting off the bad part and getting rid of it. It applies to fruit, not to people.*

As an example, I asked Luigi how he uses relevé in his technique:

> *Relevé is the wonderful feeling and excitement of dance that automatically gives me a smooth float-ing rise. It all comes from the inside. Find the inside control rather than the outside wasted energy.*

For advanced and professional dancers, feeling from the inside is a state of mind, which some call "focus" or "presence." Athletes call it "being in the zone." Here we try to feel the body dancing from the inside, to be honestly in the moment, in command of the many factors that come together at one time and one place to make art happen.

How one moves through the exercises and performs a dance must be honestly of the moment—a reflection of an inner, focused state.

> *When you look in the mirror, don't see your face, see your soul—that's what people around you see.*

Never Stop Moving

What feeling is there inside of you that wants you to move? What joy is there in moving? What motivates you to dance? You may find motivation in the music, and that's a valid reason; but it may not be digging deeply enough.

When Luigi was in that empty studio after he learned to stand and take his first halting steps, he quickly realized that he could not take just one step and collapse before he took the next one. He had to keep the flow going. He had to maintain his strength and his con-centration. He had to keep moving, even when he seemed not to be moving. This, too, is a principle of his technique. When holding a position, the body is constantly making adjustments: the shoulders are pulling down, the stomach is lifting, the weight is lifting out of the lower body. Seemingly still poses are not still; just under the sur-face, they are alive with movement. There is no downtime in a Luigi dance or exercise. The dancer is always fully engaged—the whole body and the whole mind—and must summon a great deal of energy and stamina to perform these quiet, controlled exercises.

> *The strength of the simplicity makes it beautiful.*

By being totally focused on your own body, you retain control and cannot be injured. Luigi is very proud that no one has been injured in his classes. In fact, professional dancers come to his class when they are injured.

> *If it feels right on the inside, it will be right on the outside.*

Dancing Inside the Circle

> *Balanchine spoke about dancing inside a square. I go beyond the square and dance inside a circle.*

Having said this, Luigi walks to the mirrors, stands facing them, about two feet away, and puts his arms in second position, his fingertips lightly touching the mirror. As he moves them up to third, fourth, and high fifth positions, his fingertips never leave the mirror.

> *Use the strength of your back from fingertip to fingertip. If I had paint on my fingertips, I would be tracing circles on the mirrors.*

Then he moves to center floor and says:

> *if I painted my feet, you would see a precise pattern on the floor. The feet move side, front, diagonal, and back. The movement is initiated from the inside, but it goes out in precise directions in space.*

Luigi's technique is timeless. His floor patterns are as intricate and precise as those of a Renaissance dance. Dance historians may note in the photographs that follow how Luigi's arm positions are exactly those of Noverre or Pavlova: rounded and forward and in harmony with the shape of the body.

Though you can learn the technique and work the exercises at your own pace, it is not an easy technique. It will take time for you to develop the stamina necessary to perform all the exercises with the focused attention that is the goal.

> *As you strengthen your focus, you strengthen your spine.*

The physical, psychological, and spiritual rewards of mastering these exercises are worth the effort.

Neither is this a self-indulgent technique. It is classical in its rigor and precision. In fact, Luigi sometimes compares his positions to musical notes and expects his dancers to hit them with perfect pitch, "not too flat or too sharp, but right on." Second-position arms is a good example. They shouldn't be too high or too low, or too far back or forward. There is a perfect place for them to be in relation to the body, and it's on the imaginary barre. *As you press down on that barre, you are feeling the position from the inside. As you feel that position over and over again, you learn to hit it cleanly—with perfect pitch.*

> *Technique is like tuning an instrument: Learn to tune your body just right so that when you go to play it, it's beautiful.*

For the Student

This technique is a profoundly rich system that Luigi developed over nearly a half-century, with the following goals:

- To train the dancer to stand, balance, and move out into space

- To heal and protect the dancer's body from injury

- To help the dancer dance to and with jazz music

As you move through Part Two of this book, keep these goals in mind. First, read Luigi's explanation of what each exercise series is designed to teach. (He is very specific about the goals of each exercise.) Then look at the movement implied by the photos as they dance across the page. Transitions from one photographed position to the next should be direct and clean. Finally, read the step-by-step instructions. You will find repetition of certain concepts: these are the basic tenets of the technique, without knowledge of which you will not progress.

Once you understand what you are trying to achieve and how to go about achieving it, put on the music and look inside yourself. These exercises should feel wonderful, even joyful. You should not feel pain or twinges or pulling; be especially careful of the joints— muscles stretch willingly; joints don't and shouldn't.

There is no ideal body type for this dance style; each dancer makes the technique his or her own. Beginners can, and should, move through the exercises at their own speed and at their own level. Luigi has these recommendations:

Because complete concentration is both desirable and necessary, it will be better to learn each exercise series individually rather than trying to do all of them at once. Begin with the pre-warm up; do it over and over again, until it becomes natural; then move on to the next series. The pre-warm up is an excellent, though less intense, warm up; and it should be done daily—especially as preparation for other classes or physical activities.

The technique works. It has been refined over a long period—on Luigi's body, on his students' bodies, on the bodies of his students' students. As you learn the technique and start to feel comfortable with it, you will experience moments of complete understanding, "Aha!" moments when the depth of the technique is revealed. Luigi says:

> *Now, why are these exercises spaced as they are spaced? Okay, I didn't do this right away. It took forty-some years to space these exercises, and I'm still re-ordering them. I'm finding different ways with spacing them from time to time as I find out more about my body. When you do the same exercises all the time, you will find more things to find out about your body than by doing a lot of different exercises and becoming confused. If you do one exercise right, it's better than doing a lot of exercises all mish-moshed all wrong.*

Perhaps now you will understand why we emphasize Luigi's personal story, his accident and rehabilitation, his background and experience in a book about his dance technique. It is because, as Luigi says, the exercises are the story of his life, and it is by understanding Luigi that you will understand his exercises and be open to his gift.

When you understand that these exercises were developed from physical and artistic necessity, you will understand that, for you to develop, you have to look inside yourself, as Luigi did. Find out, from inside, what this warm up is teaching you. As you change from position to position what feels good, what doesn't work, sense where your center of balance is, how the weight shifts to move forward, side, back, and diagonally. Focus on the adjustments you must continually make (*"never stop moving"*) for balance, control, comfort, line. It's a simple technique, really: Feel the exercises from the inside, so you can feel the dance from the inside.

Luigi, on Music

My technique started in the late 40's and early 50's. At that time, it was the music of the day that I liked. When I began teaching, it was always with live musicians. I always thought of my body as another instrument. In class, the live musicians followed my body. This is when I realized that my body has a melodic, lyrical flow. I liked this and followed it through. I immediately recorded my own exercise records, and here, again, the musicians followed my body. My body conducted the music.

Later, I began to use records, tapes, etc., in class, but I seldom liked vocalists, because I found myself listening to words rather than music. When dancing, I still use the first "Mission Impossible" music by Lalo Schifrin, "Masterpiece" by the Temptations, Aaron Copland's "Theme for the Common Man." I also use Duke Ellington's records, especially "Night Creatures," Dizzy Gillespie's "Manteca," and Count Basie's "Satin Doll." I love most big band music, from Glenn Miller to Artie Shaw, from "Sing, Sing, Sing" to "Moonlight Serenade."

If you're doing jazz, use the good stuff—legendary musicians, of course. I don't use rap or funk music because the beat is too loud and steady. I like music with more variation of sound and, again, I'm not too crazy about lyrics, which rap and funk have. I love the music from MGM musicals, and, of course, George Gershwin and Cole Porter. If I use a lyric song, I like Ella Fitzgerald, Nat King Cole, or Tony Bennett. These singers give me a "soul" feeling.

I've just finished a new exercise cassette and CD, called "Luigi," conducted and composed by Johnny Varro. Check for release with Princeton Book Company, Publishers, P.O. Box 57, Pennington, New Jersey 08534; or Francis Roach, at 71 West 68th Street, New York, New York 10023.

Each exercise is the story of my life.
I use them to dance and to live.

Part Two

THE
EXERCISES

PRE-WARM UP

The pre-warm up loosens and wakes up the body. It helps you to tune in to your body here and now. It teaches you how to strengthen the body, by putting it in the right positions, and builds stamina, without forcing. What you learn about the body in the pre-warm up, you apply to every other exercise in the technique, because it introduces you to yourself from the inside.

I developed this first exercise for my own therapy. I felt that I could not just walk into a dance class and start without some preparation or warm up of my own. I used this exercise when I was teaching ballet classes. I found out that many people liked, and also needed, this warm up. Later, when I created my jazz technique, I kept this exercise in and called it a "pre-warm up," feeling that it gets the body prepared for the more complicated exercises that follow, and that it helps prevent injury.

Let's begin by putting the body in the right starting position: stand with the legs apart in a comfortable, natural position and feel the feet solid to the ground. Use a natural turn-out of the hips and legs, with the knees over the toes (second position). A turn-out should be developed, not forced. Center the body, with your weight distributed evenly on both legs, and lift the weight above the hips. Place the palms on the front of the hips, with the elbows pressing forward. Now apply the basics of my technique: pull in the stomach, tighten the buttocks, and pull the shoulders down. Keep the shoulders down without pulling them back, open across the back, and think of lifting the head from the back of the ears, as the chin goes in toward the body.

Standing in this position, you can imagine a straight line going up from the anus through the spine to the top of the head. This is the center line of the body. I like to feel that imaginary line going up, up, up, as if I'm connected to something higher that is always lifting me up. It reminds you to always keep the upper part of the body suspended so that you don't overdevelop or injure the lower part of the body.

Remember, even when the body stands still, it never stops moving, never stops moving, never stops moving....

Stretch Right, Stretch Left, Plié, and Up

1. The starting position.

2. From the back, press the right arm down to second position.

3. Continue stretching the right arm over the head, with the shoulders down. Reach the right side up, allowing the rib cage to shift right. Shift the pelvis and hips comfortably to the left, and bend the right knee as far as you can, while keeping the knee over the toes and the heel down into the floor (demi-plié).

4.   Repeat on the other side, reaching the left arm up, shifting the rib cage left and hips right, with a demi-plié on the left leg. Remember to keep pulling in the stomach muscles.

5.   Repeat the first stretch; reach the right side up, pulling the shoulders down, and keep the arms rounded and reaching.

6.   Reach the left side up, hips right; and demi-plié left. Try not to shift the weight from side to side, but continue stretching up, as if climbing a rope.

[4]

[5]

[6]

[7]

[8]

The reaching-up exercise is combined with rounding the back and bending the knees to release the stiffness in the body.

7. Continue by pressing the arms to second position, and open the muscles across the back. Feel the feet solid to the ground without rolling the weight too far in or out.

8. Keeping the knees over the toes, stretch open the inner thighs into a lower, comfortable bend, with the heels on the floor (second-position grand plié). Keep the spine straight, and press the stomach into the back and the hips forward, to prevent arching the back.

9. Hold the thighs open, pull the hips back, and reach the arms forward. Then press the chin toward the chest and round the shoulders; release the hips—stretching from the tailbone to the base of the skull (roll-down).

10. Pull the stomach muscles in. This will round and support the spine while straightening the back. Align the vertebrae one over the other, straightening to a standing position. Allow the legs to straighten automatically, and press the pelvis forward. Feel the muscles stretch open across the back into the hands and fingertips.

[9]

[10]

COUNTS

PREPARATION	Stand in a natural second position, hands pressing on hip bones [1]
AND	Press right arm through second position to fifth [2]
1, 2	Stretch right [3]
3, 4	Stretch left [4]
5, 6	Stretch right [5]
7, 8	Stretch left [6]
1, 2	Hips back, arms forward, roll down [7, 8]
3, 4	Grand plié; press arms to second position [9]
5, 6, 7, 8	Roll up, straighten legs naturally [10]

REPEAT 3 more times.

Reach Through—Side View

The next movement continues the rounding exercise to loosen the muscles in the back without overstretching. As the arms reach through the legs during the roll-up, feel the fingertips continuing to press back against the space.

[11]

[12]

11. Pull the shoulders down, suck in the stomach and tighten the buttocks. Lift the upper part of the body from the lower part.

12. Keep the upper part of the body lifted, and bend both legs into a grand plié, pressing the arms down and through the legs. Then round the shoulders; press the chin toward the chest, and drop the hips.

13. Pull the stomach muscles in to roll up, pressing the arms forward of the body. The legs straighten slowly; feel the muscles stretch across the back into the fingertips.

14. Continue to lengthen the spine, pulling the shoulders down and lifting the stomach muscles up under the rib cage as the legs straighten.

[13]

[14]

COUNTS

1, 2	Plié in second position [11]
3, 4	Hips back; reach arms through legs [12]
5, 6, 7, 8	Roll up [13–14]

REPEAT 3 more times.

Shoulder Roll

This movement helps the body to achieve better posture. If a person's shoulders are too far forward, they need to pull back without arching the back. If the shoulders are too far back, or are lifted up, they need to pull forward and down. The demi-plié develops the muscles in the legs, and the half-toe is a matter of style—a feeling of jazz dance line.

[15]

[16]

[17]

15. Keeping the weight above the hips, shift the balance to the right side, lifting the left heel up as the ball of the left foot presses into the floor (half-toe position).

16. Keep the spine straight, and pull the shoulders down to start a circling movement, with a demi-plié of both legs.

17. Roll the shoulders and arms forward of the body, and slowly lift the body up from the demi-plié.

18.　Continue rolling the shoulders up, straightening both legs; tighten the buttocks to press the hips forward.

19.　Roll the shoulders back and down to complete a circle.

[18]

[19]

COUNTS

and	Left heel up [15]
1	Shoulders press down, demi-plié [16]
2	Shoulders forward, demi-plié [17]
3	Shoulders up, legs straighten [18]
4	Shoulders roll back and down [19]

REPEAT 3 more times.

REVERSE (back, up, forward, down) and REPEAT 4 times.

25

Right Arm Up and Out, Then Left

This movement uses the feeling of pressing out against space with your whole body. Keeping the shoulders down, use the back as if pressing something away.

[20]

[21]

[22]

[23]

20. Lift the back to shift the rib cage left and the hips right. Place the left hand on the hip, with the elbow forward: the right arm presses to second position. Demi-plié the left leg, keeping the knees over the toes and the feet solid to the ground.

21. Press the right arm high, with the shoulder down.

22. Pull the right elbow down near the rib cage, and flex the wrist.

23. Press out through the space to the natural alignment of the arm in second position: shoulder down, elbow lower and slightly curved, palm and fingertips even lower and pressing down.

24. Repeat on the other side, shifting the rib cage right, the hips left. Demi-plié the right leg; lift the upper body away from the lower part, suspending the weight above the hips, for a "no-weight-down" feeling. Press the left arm high, with the shoulder down.

25. Pull the left elbow down, flexing the wrist.

26. Press out against the space to second position.

[24]

[25]

[26]

COUNTS

1, 2	Rib cage left, hips right, press right arm up [20, 21]
3, 4	Flex right arm down, and press out to second position through fingertips [22, 23]

REPEAT 3 more times.

1, 2	Press left arm up [24, 25]
3, 4	Press out to second [26]

REPEAT 3 more times.

Both Arms Up and Press Down

This movement teaches a new direction of the body and moving smoothly from one position to the next.

[27]

[28]

[29]

27. Press both arms up, keeping the shoulders down. Shift the rib cage left and the hips right; demi-plié the left leg.

28. Pull the elbows down near the rib cage, flexing the palms.

29. Press the palms and fingertips down to a natural side position, feeling the shoulders drop down. Then the back lifts up, bringing the torso center; and the legs straighten.

30. Repeat, pressing the arms up and straightening the legs. Shift the rib cage right and the hips left. Demi-plié the right leg.

31. Keep the body lifted while pulling the elbows down and flexing the wrists.

32. Press the hands down to the sides. Then straighten the body to return center.

[32]

[31]

[30]

COUNTS

1, 2	Outside circle arms, rib cage left, hips right, left plié [27]
3	Elbows down, flex wrists [28]
4	Arms pressing down through space [29]
5, 6	Arms up, shift rib cage right, hips left, right plié [30]
7	Elbows down, flex wrists [31]
8	Shoulders down, complete pressing down [32]

REPEAT 1 more time.

Rib Cage

This movement teaches lifting the upper part of the body away from the lower part of the body, using the stomach (abdominal) muscles. By learning how not to drop the weight of the upper body down, you protect the small of the back, hips, legs, and feet from injury.

Also, learn to never separate the body. The word isolation does not pertain to the body because the whole body works together and never stops moving.

[33]

33. Pull the stomach in, press the shoulders down, and tighten the buttocks. Feel the feet solid to the ground, and pull up on the thigh muscles. Press the arms to second position. Use the space as your barre.

34. Lift the back and shift the rib cage right, without moving the hips or legs.

35. Return the rib cage to center.

36. Continue to lift the back; shift the rib cage left, then center.

[34]

[35]

[36]

COUNTS

AND	Center, arms in second [33]
1	Rib cage right [34]
2	Center [35]
3	Rib cage left [36]
4	Center [35]

REPEAT 3 more times.

CONTINUE, passing through center and doubling the counts.

1, 3, 5, 7	Rib cage right [34]
2, 4, 6, 8	Rib cage left [36]

REPEAT 1 more time.

31

First Break

This break is a shift to a new position, using the feet in a natural turn-out I call the "V position." Standing with the heels together and the toes slightly apart teaches you to step out to the side, leading, with the toes pointing, to the natural turn-out used in jazz.

[37]

[38]

37. Lengthen the spine and pull the stomach in. Demi-plié the right leg, with "no weight down."

38. Using the armpits, press down against your imaginary barre in second position, to shift the balance onto the left leg. Point the right foot, with the heel turning forward.

39. Press the heels together and toes slightly apart in the V position; demi-plié both legs, pressing the thighs together. Then round the back and press the chin down as the arms drop down. Place the hands in front of the hips, almost touching, with the elbows slightly curved (first-position arms).

40. Pull the stomach in and roll up, lengthening the back. Press the arms high, with the shoulders down and the elbows slightly curved (fifth-position arms), while the legs straighten automatically.

41. Press the arms open to second position; then repeat, pressing the knees and thighs together in demi-plié.

[39]

[40]

[41]

COUNTS

1, 2	Plié right [37]
3, 4, 5, 6	Back lengthens, arms press down, straighten both legs, point right low [38]
7, 8	V position; plié, round the spine, arms press to first position [39]
1, 2, 3, 4	Roll up, legs straighten, arms press to fifth position [40]
5, 6, 7, 8	Arms press to second; plié [41]

Press Forward and Pull Away

This movement takes the body in a side direction while the head and body are still facing front. The hip leads into the direction while the rib cage pulls away. I use the rib cage for a couple of reasons. One, for direction; and two, to protect the hip muscles. There are many people who think that the jazziest thing is the pelvis. I think of my rib cage. I free the pelvis to move where it's going beautifully.

[42]

[43]

[44]

[45]

42. Pull the stomach in; straighten the legs and press the arms forward, dropping the chin down.

43. Lift the back and shift the rib cage left while pressing the arms down through first to second position, with the right shoulder slightly forward. Demi-plié both legs without rolling the knees or ankles in or out.

44. Bring the rib cage center. Press the arms forward again.

45. Shift the rib cage to the right and the arms to second. Bring the left side forward. Demi-plié both legs.

46. Return the rib cage center again, straightening the legs.

47. Press the arms through first position; shift the rib cage left to "pull away" the weight from your opposite hip and leg. Step out into second position with the right leg; lead with the hip. Demi-plié both legs while keeping both shoulders and hips "square" (facing front).

48. Return to center; reverse.

49. Repeat the pull-away, with the rib cage right, stepping out with the left leg to the V position.

[46]

[47]

[48]

[49]

COUNTS

1, 2	Legs straighten; arms forward [42]
3, 4	Arms first to second; plié [43]
5, 6	Legs straight, arms forward [44]
7, 8	Arms in, plié [45]

REPEAT 1 more time.

1, 2	Center, open the back, legs straighten [46]
3, 4	Rib cage left, hips right, open to second plié [47]
5, 6	Center, stomach in, arms forward [48]
7, 8	Rib cage right, hips left, second plié [49]

REPEAT 1 more time.

Break into Close-Lock Fourth
And Epaulement

*This break is a weight change into a balance, then a powerful align-
ment position I call "close-lock fourth." A close-lock fourth position is
a closed fourth position from ballet adapted to jazz. With both legs
in plié, one knee is in back of the other, locking them together by lifting the back heel off the ground. The weight is distributed equally
on both legs and lifted above the hips. The front foot is solid to the
ground. The inner thighs press together from the knees to the buttocks, to keep the hips in alignment and pressed forward so as not
to arch the back.*

*The épaulement is the use of the shoulders and upper body that
gives balance and direction for the body to move in. I describe this
simply as the rhythm of the body, the feeling in which you get there.*

[50]

[51]

[52]

[53]

[54]

50.   Pull the stomach into the back to lift up off the left plié and right hip. Straighten both legs and point the left foot, with the heel pressing forward. Press the left arm fifth and the right arm second, with the shoulders down.

51.   Half-circle back, with the straight left leg pointed on the floor *(rond de jambe)* or lifted comfortably in the air *(rond de jambe en l'air)*. Keep the weight up and the back straight. Step back, distributing the weight equally between both straight legs; one leg is in back of the other, with a comfortable open space in between and the heels down (fourth position). Plié through fourth position, shifting the weight back onto the left leg; stretch-point the right leg.

52.   Turn the hips and shoulders square to the front; lift the left heel, press the left knee inside the back of the right, and demi-plié. Squeeze the thighs together (close-lock fourth position). Lift the upper part of the body out of the lower.

53.   The left arm circles inside and down, pressing through first.

54.   Press left arm to second position; square the shoulders front.

55. Pull the stomach up, and press the right side forward, controlling the arms on the imaginary barre. Use the back and chest equally, pressing forward through the space without rounding the shoulders or arching the back. Look straight forward (focus) without turning the head.

56. Repeat épaulement on the left side.

[55]

[56]

COUNTS

1, 2, 3, 4	Balance on right leg, left arm fifth, right second, point left [50]
5, 6, 7, 8	Half-circle left leg back, plié fourth, point right leg [51]
1, 2, 3, 4	Pivot front, plié in close-lock fourth [52]
5, 6, 7, 8	Inside circle left arm to second, hips forward (53, 54)
1, 2	Right épaulement, press into fingertips [55]
3, 4	Left épaulement [56]
5, 6	Repeat right [55]
7, 8	Repeat left [56]

REPEAT the last eight counts 3 more times.

Break into Close-Lock Fourth
And Jazz Arms

The break on the right side again repeats the weight change into close-lock fourth. The arms follow classical positions and are taken from the jazz choreography Luigi learned on Hollywood's movie sets. Press the arms from the center of the back. Reach out natural-ly, moving the arms in line and following the path of the body from one position to the next.

[57]

[58]

57.   Stand in second position, and pull the stomach into the back, with the shoulders down. Lift the right heel up, shift-ing the balance onto the left side. Point the right foot, press-ing the heel forward and touching the toes on the floor (tendu). Press the right arm to fifth position and the left to second.

58.   Half-circle the right leg back to a croisé fourth-position plié. Shift the weight back onto the right leg, and point the left foot front. Plié through fourth again, and shift the weight forward.

59.   Turn the hips and shoulders square front into close-lock fourth position.

60.   Circle the right arm inside and down, pressing through first position.

61.   Press the right arm to second position; square the shoulders.

[60]

[59]

[61]

COUNTS

1, 2, 3, 4	Balance on left leg, right arm fifth, point right toe [57]
5, 6, 7, 8	Half-circle right leg back, plié fourth, point left foot [58]
1, 2, 3, 4	Pivot front, plié in close-lock [59]
5, 6, 7, 8	Left arm circles inside, first to second [60, 61]

[62]

[63]

[64]

[65]

62. Press the palms in toward the belt line, the elbows out to the side and forward of the body.

63. Pull the elbows down, and press the palms to the shoulders.

64. Reach the arms straight up, with the shoulders down; lift the body to straighten the legs.

65. Press the right shoulder forward as both arms reach out and down to second position. Plié in close-lock fourth.

66. Press the palms in.

67. Pull the elbows down.

68. Reach the arms straight up while both legs straighten.

69. The left shoulder presses forward as the arms press out and down to second; the legs are in close-lock fourth.

70. Press the palms in.

71. Pull the elbows down.

[66]

[67]

[68]

[69]

[70]

[71]

72. Reach straight up as both legs straighten, and point the right leg to second.

73. Press the right shoulder forward while reaching the arms out, then down, to second position.

74. Bring the right leg back into close-lock fourth position.

[72]

[73]

[74]

75. Press the palms in.

76. Pull the elbows down.

77. Reach both arms up, shift the balance back, placing the right heel down; touch-point the left foot to open the second position.

[75]

[76]

[77]

[78]

[79]

[80]

78. Press the left shoulder and left hip slightly forward (effacé), as the arms press down to second. Pull the stomach in, press down on the armpits, and tighten the buttocks. Raise the body up until the right heel automatically lifts off the floor, shifting the weight onto the ball of the foot (relevé). Keep the left toes guiding on the floor.

79. Press the right shoulder forward. Then bend, and lift the left knee, turning it close to the right leg (turned-in passé). (Whenever a foot is off the ground, point the foot for more strength and a good dance line.)

80. Continue pressing the right side forward. Pass the left leg over the right and step down, rolling through the left foot, pressing forward (degage) into close-lock fourth position.

COUNTS

1, 2	Press palms to belt line, elbows forward [62]
3, 4	Elbows down, palms up [63]
5, 6	Arms up, legs straighten, right heel up [64]
7, 8	Reach right side forward, arms second, close-lock [65]
1, 2	Press palms in, shoulders down [66]
3, 4	Elbows down, hips forward [67]
5, 6	Press arms up, legs straighten, right heel up [68]
7, 8	Reach left side forward, arms second, close-lock [69]

REPEAT 1 more time.

AND, A	Elbows out; elbows down [70, 71]
1, 2, 3, 4	Press arms up, legs straighten, point right second [72]
5, 6	Press right, arms second, lift right leg [73]
7, 8	Passé back, close-lock, right side forward [74]
AND, A	Elbows out, elbows down, right heel down [75, 76]
1, 2, 3, 4	Press arms up, balance on right, point left second [77]
5, 6	Arms press second, left side forward, slow relevé [78]
7	Right shoulder forward, turned-in passé left [79]
8	Complete degage forward, close-lock fourth [80]

REPEAT 1 more time.

Relax, Then Reach Through

This movement teaches balance and increases flexibility.

[81]

[82]

81. Open the legs to second position and round the body down, with the arms in fifth position. Demi-plié both legs and press the chin against the chest.

82. Pull the stomach in and roll up, aligning the vertebrae.

83. Lengthen the back; straighten the legs and press the arms up to fifth position, with the shoulders down.

84. Round the back forward and down, with the arms reaching back through the legs in grand plié. Press the chin down and stretch the fingertips, pressing back through the space.

85. Pull the stomach in, and roll up.

86. Center the body, and lengthen the back with the arms in fifth.

87. Pull the stomach in, press the arms down to second position, lift up into the base of the skull, tighten the buttocks, and pull up on the thighs to relevé. Press the heels forward.

[83]

[84]]

[85]

[86]

[87]

COUNTS

1, 2, 3, 4	Round down, demi-plié [81]
5, 6, 7	Roll up, stomach in [82]
8	Straighten, arms fifth [83]

REPEAT 3 more times [84–86], then break.

1–6	Arms second, slow relevé [87]
7, 8	Heels down

49

Lift Up and Side-Stretch

The side-stretch lifts the rib cage up and away from the hips and loosens the muscles in the side, taking the body for the first time in a new direction of stretching.

[88]

[89]

[90]

88. Press the right arm to fifth position.

89. Lengthen the back and stretch side, reaching the right side over. Keep the shoulders down, and feel the muscles stretch from the right fingertips down through the right leg.

90. Demi-plié the right leg, and circle the right arm inside and down to first position.

91. Shift the rib cage back to center, straightening both legs. Then stretch-point the left foot and press the arms to second position, with the left shoulder slightly forward.

92. Bring the left leg back to close-lock fourth position.

COUNTS

1	Lift spine, right arm in fifth, shoulders down [88]
2	Right side-stretch, lift neck [89]
3, 4	Demi-plié right, circle right arm to first [90]
5, 6	Straighten, balance on right, point left, left shoulder forward, arms in second [91]
7, 8	Turn out, passé left leg back to close-lock fourth [92]

REPEAT right and left 4 times altogether.

Double up the timing of the counts without the close-lock back:

1	Center, legs second, right arm high [88]
2	Right side-stretch [89]
3	Demi-plié right, arm to first position [90]
4	Center, arms in second [35]
5	Left arm high
6	Left side-stretch
7	Left demi-plié
8	Center, arms second [35]

REPEAT double time, right and left, 1 more time.

[91]

[92]

Turn Down

This movement is a turn toward the diagonal, pulling the stomach into the back to support the straight back and to prevent it from arching. The arms are kept forward of the back in second position, with the shoulders down. The body is kept in line, inside both legs, without curving the spine over one leg.

[93]

[94]

[95]

[96]

[97]

[98]

93. Keeping the spine straight, pivot on the right half-toe to turn the body to the left diagonal.

94. Press the hips back; pull up on the thighs as the left heel drops down and the back goes forward.

95. Lift the back and the right heel.

96. Turn to center, pressing the arms to first position and dropping the right heel.

97. Lift the left heel to left half-toe, and turn to the right diagonal.

98. Press the back forward, and drop the left heel.

99. Lift the back and left heel up.

100. Return to center.

101. Press the hips back and the back forward; pull in the stomach; and pull up on the thighs, with the arms in second.

102. Lift up to center and press the right épaulement forward, with the arms in first position. Try not to turn the hips or ankles by lifting the weight above the hips.

103. Repeat, pressing the back forward; repeat, lifting to center. Then press the left épaulement forward.

[99]

[100]

COUNTS

1, 2	Turn chest and hips left, right heel up [93]
3, 4	Hips back, heel down [94]
5, 6	Lift the back, right heel up [95]
7, 8	Center, arms in first position, heel down [96]
1, 2	Turn chest and hips right, left heel up [97]
3, 4	Hips back, heel down [98]
5, 6	Lift the back; left heel up [99]
7, 8	Center, heels down [100]
1, 2	Hips back, arms second [101]
3, 4	Lift back, press right shoulder forward [102]
5, 6	Hips back, arms second [101]
7, 8	Lift the back, press, left shoulder forward [103]

REPEAT 1 more time.

[101]

[102]

[103]

Break into Circle Around

The last movement of the pre-warm up is another direction for the body—a circling movement. Guide with your whole body to follow the path.

[104]

[105]

104. Lift the body, shifting the rib cage to the left, the hips right, and pressing the right arm to second position. Then demi-plié the left leg, pressing the thigh open.

105. Press the right arm to fifth position, the left arm in front of the chest, with the shoulders down (third-position arms).

106. Pull the stomach in and lift the back off the straightening legs. Lift the left heel as the right arm guides from the top of the circle.

107. Follow a half-circle down, rounding the back and dropping the left heel into second position. Reach both arms into fifth position, and drop the chin toward the chest.

108. Complete the circle by switching the left arm to guide the body up to center. Shift the rib cage right, hips left, and right leg to demi-plié, while the arms press to third position.

[106]

[107]

[108]

COUNTS

1–8	Shift rib cage left, demi-plié, right arm second [104]
1–8	Press right arm fifth, left arm swings front [105]
1, 2	Back lifts up, stomach in, point left [106]
3, 4, 5	Half-circle down, arms fifth [107]
6, 7, 8	Complete circle left [108]

REPEAT left 1 effacé more time; then REPEAT right and left circles again.

Continue in double time:

1, 2, 3, 4	Lift back [106], circle down [107], complete circle [108]
5, 6, 7, 8	Circle to right

The pre-warm up finishes with a relevé and balance on one leg into close-lock fourth position.

[109]

[110]

109. Straighten both legs, and shift the weight onto the right side, pointing the left foot. Press the left side forward to éfacee as the arms press through first to second position.

110. Lift the back and press down into the armpits. *Use your space as your barre.* Stretch-point the left leg back, and slowly relevé on the right leg to half-toe.

111. Press the right shoulder forward, and turn in the left leg.

112. Complete stepping over, and press the left heel forward into close-lock fourth position.

[112]

[111]

COUNTS

1, 2, 3, 4	Shift to balance right, point left [109]
5, 6, 7, 8	Press left shoulder and hip front, arms second [110]
5, 6	Right shoulder forward, left knee turned in [111]
7, 8	Step over left, close-lock fourth [112]

CHEST AGAINST THE THIGHS

The Chest Against the Thighs exercise gives you complete flexibility and elasticity of the body. Formerly called "The Bounce," I renamed it to emphasize the importance of keeping the chest pressing against the thighs and the knees bent during the exercise. This position teaches you to stretch the back of the thighs and the Achilles tendons without forcing the legs straight. Also, it prevents any knee injury because the backs of the knees are not strained.

By rounding the back with the chin down, you lengthen the spine from the base of the skull to the tailbone. This helps to loosen the muscles that support the vertebrae, rather than tightening them, which can injure the disks and nerves.

113. Stand with the feet apart and aligned with the shoulders and hips; the toes are front.

114. Press the chin against the chest, and round the shoulders to roll down. Pull the hips back, demi-plié, and reach the arms forward, pressing the fingertips against the floor.

115. Press the chest against the front of the thighs, and the back of the thighs against the calves while lifting the heels. The arms are on the outside of the legs, and the weight is distributed equally in the body, keeping pressure off the knees.

[115]

[114]

[113]

116. Lift the hips up and press the heels down.

117. Keeping the chest on the thighs, stretch the hamstring and back muscles.

118. Grab hold of the ankles; keep pressing the chest against the thighs in demi-plié as the elbows press front.

119. Lift the back to straighten half-way up and straighten the legs. The back position is parallel to the floor, without arching.

[118]

[117]

[116]

[121]

[120]

[119]

120. Round the back; press the chin against the chest and demi-plié, with the heels down.

121. Pull in the stomach muscles to roll up. Stretch the muscles open across the back into the fingertips. Press the hips forward, and tighten the buttocks while straightening the legs. Lengthen the roll-up through the upper back and into the base of the skull.

122. Pull the shoulders down; hold the stomach into the back and squeeze the buttocks. Never stop moving.

[122]

COUNTS

Starting position: Feet apart in parallel position

5, 6, 7, 8   Roll down, fingertips on the floor, chest against the thighs, heels up [113–115]

AND   Lift hips up [116]

1   Release the hips down [115]

AND   Lift hips up [116]

2   Release hips down [115]

3, 4   Hips up, heels down, grab the ankles, elbows forward, chest against thighs [117]

REPEAT 7 more times. Then hold the plié an extra 4 counts [118]

Last part: Release and roll up:

1, 2   Back and legs straighten [119]

3, 4   Bend knees, chest against thighs [120]

5, 6, 7   Roll up, chin down [121]

8   Lengthen the spine [122]

THE PLIES

The pliés are basically done to develop the muscles in the legs. Also, they are designed to teach you how to keep the body weight lifted while bending down and up.

I feel that pliés are not only for the legs; a good plié develops the whole body.

It's the use of the upper part of the body that controls the pliés without overdeveloping or injuring the lower part. If you use the key areas of the body—stomach, shoulders, and buttocks—you learn how to pull up out of the hips, legs, ankles, and feet. When you have no control of the upper part of the body, it weakens the lower, because you drop the weight and sink into the knees and ankles. The pelvis pulls back and you sit into the hips and legs. When you do any plié—especially the deep kneebend called grand plié—lift the upper part of the body away and press the pelvis forward.

Anytime you are standing straight, be conscious of protecting the three key areas of the body. The sucked-in stomach will protect the back from injury. Pulling down on the shoulders and lengthening the spine protects from pinched nerves and injured disks; and it will give you a suspended feeling of lifting up. Tightening the buttocks teaches you: to keep the pelvis forward; to pull up on the thighs, building up the muscles around the knees; to hold a turn-out to protect the legs; and to strengthen the arch and insteps, distributing the weight equally in the feet.

To prepare for any plié:

Stand with the feet solid to the ground. Let the legs turn out naturally and let the turn-out develop through the exercise, never forcing it. Keep the knees always over the toes. Use the stomach, shoulders, and buttocks. Feel the back muscles open across the back and feel the space around you. Use the space as your barre.

First–Position Pliés

[123]

[124]

123. Stand with the legs straight in a comfortable turn-out from the hips. Feel the feet firm with the weight centered—neither rolling in nor out. Press the thighs, calves, and heels together (first position). Pull the shoulders down, suck in the stomach, and tighten the buttocks. Press the arms open across the back to second position.

124. Bend the elbows, and press the palms in to the belt line.

125. Lengthen the spine, and press the arms down through first position. Demi-plié, stretching the inner thighs open, with the knees over the toes and the heels pressed into the floor.

126. Keeping the back straight—with the knees turning out over the toes—bend lower, lifting the heels up; and press the thighs against the calves, with the hips pressing forward (first-position grand plié). The arms press to second position, using an imaginary barre for support.

127. Lift out of the grand plié by pulling the stomach muscles in to lift the back. Roll down through the feet, pressing through the heels to first position.

[125]

[126]

128. Straighten the legs, tighten the buttocks, and press the palms in, with the elbows out.

129. Press the arms through first position and demi-plié, stretching open the inner thighs.

130. Pull in the stomach, press down the shoulders, and straighten the legs. Press the arms out to second position.

131. Lift up from the base of the skull, and relevé with the heels pressing forward. Use the space as your barre and open across the back, as if you have one long arm from fingertip to fingertip.

[129]

[128]

[127]

[131]

[130]

COUNTS

5, 6, 7, 8	Stomach in; tighten buttocks; shoulders down; legs in first position; arms second [123]
AND	Press the palms in, elbows forward [124]
1, 2, 3, 4	Demi-plié, press arms down through first [125]
5, 6, 7, 8	Grand plié, press arms second, lengthen spine [126]
1, 2, 3, 4	Lower heels, lift the back, arms to first [127]
5, 6, 7, 8	Squeeze buttocks, thighs, and calves together— palms in, elbows forward [128]
1, 2, 3, 4	Demi-plié, arms first [129]
5, 6, 7, 8	Straighten, arms second [130]
1–6	Relevé; "your space is your barre" [131]
7, 8	Lower heels [131]

REPEAT the previous 4 eight counts for each plié series (120 counts altogether). Continue in second [132–139], "L" position (140–148), and fifth [149–156].

Second–Position Pliés

[132]

[133]

[134]

132. Stand with the feet firmly on the ground in second position.

133. Press the palms in to the belt line, with the elbows forward.

134. Keeping alignment, open thighs in a second-position grand plié. Keep the knees over the toes.

135–139. In second position, keep the heels on the floor to repeat the grand plié and demi-plié exercise: grand plié, demi-plié, and relevé.

[135]

[136]

[137]

[138]

[139]

"L" Position Pliés

[140]

[141]

[142]

Notice the photo of good posture and alignment in figure 140:
The stomach is into the back; the shoulders are down; and buttocks are tightened, with the muscles "open across the back" without pressing the shoulders back. The chest is forward.

140. Keep the left foot in second position; turn the shoulders and
      hips to the left diagonal, bringing the right heel to the
      instep. Squeeze the buttocks, thighs, and calves together.

141–147. Lifting the heels in the "L" position, grand plié exercise. Continue into the demi-plié, and relevé as before, using the same counts as for first and second pliés.

[145]

[144]

[143]

148. Pivot the body front, squaring shoulders and hips equally in line. Press the heels down into a comfortable and unforced turn-out of the hips, legs, and feet. Crossing one leg over the other, press the heel of the front leg to the toes of the back leg, with the toes turning out to the sides (fifth position). Straighten the legs, squeeze the inner thighs together, and tighten the buttocks.

[146]

[147]

[148]

Fifth–Position Pliés

[149]

[150]

149–153. The fifth-position pliés are the same as first-, second-,
and 'L" position pliés, with a slight change of arms to
fifth position to control the balance of the grand plié.

[151]

[152]

[153]

154. Press the arms down through first position, and demi-plié.

155. Guide the right leg forward, with toes on the floor. Shift the weight front, while straightening both legs. Stretch-point back through the left leg, and reach the arms to fifth position, adjusting the shoulders down and level.

156. Pull in the stomach, and keep the back straight. Roll the heels slowly up to relevé, bringing both feet to half-toe. Until the body feels the control to balance, keep both legs on the ground to help adjust the balance. Then shift the weight onto the front leg, and lift the back leg comfortably.

[155]

[154]

[156]

COUNTS

1, 2	Demi-plié [154]
3, 4	Straighten right leg, find floor behind with left toe [155]
5	Find your balance [155]
6, 7, 8	Relevé slowly [156]

FRAPPE

Frappés are exercises that teach you how to use the feet. The movement starts from a bent knee and flexed foot. As soon as the foot leaves the ground, the heel comes forward and the foot strikes the floor, then stretches through the leg to a pointed foot. The shoulders pull down to strengthen the point.

If you have any problems with the knees or ankles, use a tendu, a simple pointing movement, without striking the floor, starting with the foot flexed. If your back bothers you when this exercise goes to the back, use the tendu.

Frappé Front, Right Leg

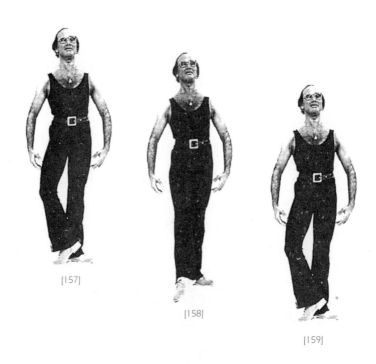

[157]

[158]

[159]

157. Lengthen the spine to balance on the left leg, and turn out the right thigh, pressing the right foot into half-toe on the floor.

158. Press the arms to second position, and brush-point the right foot forward, with the heel coming forward (frappé).

159. Brush the right foot back to center, with the heel pressing down and the toes pointing out (flexed).

[161]

[160]

[162]

160. Frappé front again, and reach the arms to fifth position.

161. Keep the stomach into the back as you demi-plié the right leg, dropping the heel down. The left leg stays straight.

162. Lift the body and shift the weight back to center, pressing the arms down to first position.

Frappé Side, Right Leg

[163]

[164]

[165]

[166]

163. Press the arms to second position, and frappé the right leg side.

164. Brush-flex the right foot in back of the left.

165. Repeat the frappé to second.

166. Brush-flex the right foot in front of the left.

167. Brush the right leg to second position, and lengthen the back as the right arm presses to fifth position. Continue into a side-stretch, with a demi-plié on the right leg.

168. Inside circle the right arm down to first position, and lift the body off the plié to return the weight to center.

169. Press the arms to second position as you brush-flex the right foot in back of the left.

[167]

[168]

[169]

Frappé Back, Right Leg—
Side and Front View

[170]

[171]

[172]

[173]

170. (Side view) Pull the stomach in to lift the back, and point-touch the right leg straight back. Keep the hips and shoulders square to the front.

171. Flexing the right foot, return the leg to center.

172. (Side view) Keeping the weight lifted, point-touch the right leg straight back into fourth position. Then plié.

173. Pull the stomach in and the shoulders down, to return to center, flexing the foot.

COUNTS

8	Balance on left leg, half-toe right [157]
1	Frappé forward, stretch-point right leg [158]
2	Flex the right foot to ankle center [159]
3	Repeat, brush forward [158]
4	Repeat the flex foot to ankle [159]
5	Brush right foot forward, arms high forward [160]
6, 7	Demi-plié right leg, right shoulder forward [161]
8	Center balance on left leg, right half-toe, arms in first position [162]

REPEAT the eight counts to second position [163–169], to fourth position [170–173], and again to second position [163–169].

Finish the frappé series by repeating to the right side, with the right leg starting from behind the left leg.

PASSE

The last part of the plié exercise series is a passé. This is a passing position of the working leg bending up and down, past the supporting leg. It teaches how to lift a bent leg straight up without shifting the balance in the body. Also, it reminds you to keep the spine straight and to use the space as your barre when you need help balancing. You can go from any other position to a passé, to test your balance and control.

[174]

[175]

174. Lengthen the spine, pull the stomach into the back, press down on the shoulders, and use the armpits to press the arms second. Bend the right knee turned out to the side, stretching open the thigh muscles (turned-out passé) and lift the right foot to the left calf, with the heel coming forward and the toes pointing back.

175. Pass the right foot in back of the left calf (passé) and down behind the Achilles tendon.

176. Passé the right foot up to the back of the left calf.

177. Passé the right foot in front of the calf, and slowly relevé on the left to half-toe.

[176]

[177]

COUNTS

1	Balance on left leg; passé right foot front [174]
2	Passé back [175–176]
3, 4	Passé front [177]
5, 6	Passé back
7, 8	Passé front

REPEAT eight counts 1 more time.

Take four counts as a break to switch the legs, and REPEAT all the frappés and passés on the left leg. Then take another four-count break to put the legs in first position again.

REPEAT the entire plié series on the right side.

FIRST PORT DE BRAS:
Eight-and-a-One

I have created three port de bras, which are more advanced movements than the other exercises. They lean more toward the classical exercises needed for the elegance and sophistication of dance. The term "port de bras," also called "adagio," implies the use of slow music with slow movements. Slow music means harder stretches. You feel the length of the music and get through to the feeling and control that is needed to move gracefully.

This is the first port de bras that starts on the rhythmic phrase, "eight-and-a-one." These counts are an upbeat phrase ahead of the downbeat found in many styles of music. I say "eight-and-a-one" as a description of the start of the exercise.

For the first time in the technique, this exercise carries you to every direction in dance: front, side, back, cross (croisé), down, up, and side.

Feel the flow of moving from one position to the next, and find the strength to do so.

178. Balance on the left leg, lifting the right heel to half-toe, with the arms in first. Pull up off the hips, being careful never to sit into one hip.

179. Press the arms to second with the elbows in front of the body. Keep the stomach pulling in, and lengthen the spine. Brush-point the right leg to the side, lifting it to a comfortable height off the floor and keeping the hips down. Then press the heel of the right foot to face front to work the leg turned out from the hip (à la seconde).

180. Press the shoulders down into the space as your barre, and touch the back of the calf, or higher, with the right foot.

181. Touch the right foot to the front of the left leg.

[178]

[179]

[180]

[181]

[182]

[183]

182. Use the armpits pressing down and the stomach into the back for more control of the balance. Stretch the right leg out to second again.

183. Lower the right leg down to touch the floor. Reach the right arm to fifth position and the left to second, with the shoulders down. Then lift the right side of the body up and over to the left side, pulling away from the right hip (side-stretch).

184. Pull the stomach in and straighten the back. Circle the right arm outside and down from first to second position, as the left arm presses inside from first to fifth. Bend the right leg, sliding the ball of the foot in to the left instep. Side-stretch left, up and over to the right.

185. The ribs pull under the chest as the arms open across the back. Pull both the shoulders down, and press the right arm in front of the body (third-position arms).

186. Lift and straighten the back.

187. Press both arms to first position.

[184]

[185]

[186]

[187]

188. Press the arms to second position, and open across the back.

189. Keep the back straight, and pull the hips back, with the stomach in. Continue to press the arms second.

190. Lift the body to center.

[188]   [189]   [190]

COUNTS

PREPARATION

5, 6, 7	Weight left, right half-toe, arms first to second [178]
8	Point right to second [179]
AND	Bend right, touch back of left leg [180]
A	Touch right foot to front of left leg [181]
1	Stretch-point right leg to second, arms second [182]
2, 3, 4	Right side-stretch, left leg stretches down [183]
5, 6, 7, 8	Center, left side-stretch, left arm fifth, right half-toe [184]
1, 2, 3, 4	Right arm forward, full side-stretch [185]
5	Pulling up to center [186]
6, 7	Center, arms first to second [187]

Eight-AND-A-ONE REPEAT, point right leg side, back, front, side
2–8, 1–7   REPEAT, side-stretch right, switch left.

8	Arms second [188]
1	Hips pull back; back is straight, arms second [189]
2	Lift the back slightly
3	Hips pull back
4	Lift the back slightly
5	Hips pull back
6, 7	Straighten [190]

REPEAT from the first eight-and-a-one movement, 1 more time.

Eight-and-a-One: Croisé

[191]

[192]

[193]

[194]

[195]

[196]

[197]

[198]

[199]

191. Turn the body toward the left diagonal, pressing the arms to first position and lifting the right heel to half-toe.

192. Brush the right foot forward to croisé, keeping the right knee bent, the heel up, and the left leg straight. Press the arms to second position, and pull the weight up out of the legs.

193. Lift the back, turn the right side out, and press the heel down.

194. Turn the right side out, and press the heel down.

195. Lift the weight up off the plié to shift back, and balance on the left leg. Open passé right. Lift the arms to fifth.

196. Hold the balance and pivot to face front. Press the right leg down to half-toe as the arms press to first position. Then press the right heel down in front of the left toes, and bring the right toes back to the left heel (fifth position). Demi-plié with both legs.

197. In plié, brush the right leg forward to fourth position, lifting the right heel up. Straighten the left leg, and press the arms to second.

198. Lift the back, and turn the right side to the left again.

199. Turn the right side out. Press the heel down to square front.

200. Pull the stomach in and the shoulders down to lift out of the right plié. Balance on the left side, with the right leg in open passé. Lift the arms to fifth position.

201. Bring the right foot down, pressing through the toes, ball, and heel into fifth position. Demi-plié with both legs, and press the arms to first position.

202. Brush the right leg to second position, lifting the right heel while straightening the left leg. Open the arms to second.

203. Lift the back and slide in again. Reach the arms forward, and lift up into the base of the skull.

[200]

[201]

[202]

[203]

[204]

[205]

204. Turn the right side out.

205. Pulling the weight up, balance on the left leg; open passé the right leg, with the arms pressing into fifth position.

COUNTS

Eight-and-a-1—Croisé:

8-AND-A-1	Right half-toe, arms first [191]
2, 3, 4	Brush right in demi-plié, arms second [192]
5, 6, 7, 8	Turn the right shoulder and knee in, heel up, lift the back [193]
1, 2	Turn out, shoulder square, heel down [194]
3, 4	Balance on left, right passé, lift the spine [195]
5, 6, 7	Pivot front, right half-toe [196]

Eight-and-a-1—Front:

8-AND-A-1	Demi-plié [196]
2, 3, 4	Brush forward right plié, arms second [197]
5, 6, 7, 8	Turn the right shoulder and knee in, heel up, lift the back [198]
1, 2	Turn out, shoulders square, heel down [199]
3, 4	Balance on left, right passé, lift the spine [200]
5, 6, 7	Right half-toe, demi-plié, arms first [201]

Eight-and-a-1—Second:

8-AND-A-1	Demi-plié [201]
2, 3, 4	Brush second right plié, heel up [202]
5, 6, 7, 8	Turn the right shoulder and knee in, heel up, lift the back [203]
1, 2, 3, 4	Turn out, shoulders square, heel down [204]

Eight-and-a-One: Forward Bow

[206]

[207]

[208]

[209]

206. Press the right leg in back to close-lock fourth position and the arms to second.

207. Turn the shoulders to the left diagonal. Then pull the hips back, press the chest forward, and bend into a grand plié.

208. Return to close-lock fourth, facing front.

209. Step the right leg back, opening to fourth-position demi-plié.

210. Pull the stomach in and shoulders down to lift off the plié; balance on the left leg, with the right leg in open passé. Press the arms to first position.

211. Stretch the right leg back to fourth position and demi-plié. Press the arms into second position. Keep the weight lifted above the hips and out of the plié.

[210]

[211]

COUNTS

1, 2, 3, 4	Right leg back close-lock fourth, arms second [206]
5, 6, 7, 8	Turn chest to diagonal; grand plié [207]
1, 2	Center close-lock [208]
3, 4	Right leg back, plié fourth [209]
5, 6	Passé right, left leg straight [210]
7	Right leg back; demi-plié fourth [211]

Eight-and-a-One: Side View

[215]

[214]

[213]

[212]

212. Lift the back, and slide the heels together in first position; straighten both legs.

213. Continue pressing the right leg through first, pointing to a straight kick (battement) front.

214. Bending the right knee, circle the right foot inside in counter-clockwise direction.

215. Extend, pointing the right leg, while pressing the hips forward with the shoulders pulling back (layout). Keep shoulders and arms down to control the landing on right leg.

216. Land the right foot forward, pressing through the toes—ball and heel—to a parallel position.

217. Pull the stomach in, and turn the right heel in.

218. Using the armpits to press down on the imaginary barre, pull the weight up to balance on the left leg; passé right.

219. Shift the weight back, with the right leg stepping back to fourth position; then demi-plié.

[218]

[217]

[216]

[219]

COUNTS

8-AND-A-	Brush heels together through first [212], and battement front [213]
1	Right thigh turned in, bend knee [214]
2	Kick out, hips forward, shoulders back (layout) [215]
3, 4	Press right foot down [216]
5	Lift back, turn out right leg [217]
6	Passé right; your space is your barre [218]
7	Plié fourth [219]

REPEAT 3 more times.

Eight-and-a-One:
Balance and Relevé

[220]

[221]

[222]

[223]

[224]

220. Balance on the left leg with the foot; the arms are in first.

221. Lift the right knee to open passé; the arms press forward.

222. Continue lifting the arms up to fifth position; extend and straighten the right leg (développé) to second position.

223. Keep lifting the weight above the hips, and press the arms to second, with the elbow in front of the leg.

224. Lift the back; the arms press to fifth position.

225. Circle the right leg.

226. Press the arms forward to second, using the stomach, shoulders, and armpits to control the balance.

227. Lift into the base of the skull and relevé on the left foot. Press down on the space as your barre.

[225]

[226]

[227]

COUNTS

Counts	Description
1, 2	Balance on left leg, right half-toe, arms first [220]
3, 4	Passé right, arms front [221]
5, 6, 7, 8	Développé right, arms fifth [222]
1, 2, 3, 4	Arms second [223]
5, 6, 7, 8	Hold balance; never stop moving [224]
1, 2	Arms fifth, right leg circles back [225]
3, 4	Right leg back, arms first to second [226]
5, 6, 7, 8	Plié fourth, point left
1, 2, 3, 4	Plié fourth, balance on left, arms second
5, 6, 7, 8	Relevé. Your space is your barre [227]

REPEAT the First Port de Bras exercise on the other side.

SECOND PORT DE BRAS

This is the logo position which has become associated with my technique. It's part of the second port de bras which is a variation of the "rhythm of the body"—a lyrical movement which teaches you how to go from one position to the next. It is a combination of exercise and dance movement that is a true feeling of dance.

This was the first exercise I ever created, and it is very defining of the Luigi style. It tells a story of the technique. Its positions are like the notes of music: the body becomes a sound.

The body moves inside of a circle, making a beautiful design from beginning to end.

[230]

[229]

[228]

228. Cross the left leg back to close-lock fourth position, with the hips square and pressing forward. Lengthen the spine out of the lower back, and press the arms to second position.

229. Press the left shoulder forward, and stretch the left arm down through first position. Shift the rib cage left and the hips right as the left leg steps out to second half-toe.

230. Keeping the shoulders down, circle the left arm inside to fifth position.

231. Lengthen the back so that the weight is above the demi-plié, and shift the rib cage left. Then press the right shoulder forward and square both shoulders.

232. Lift the body, bringing the legs to first position.

233. Pull more down on the left shoulder as the left leg brushes back, lifting the foot off the floor with the knee bent. Keep the hips down; lift the inner thigh back, turned out with the foot lower than the knee (back attitude).

234. Close-lock fourth, with the left leg back.

235. Circle the left arm down through first position to second.

236. Pull the hips back and grand plié. Round the back down, and press the arms to fifth position.

237. Pull the stomach in, lift the back, and press the arms to second.

[231]

[232]

[233]

[234]

[235]

[236]

[237]

COUNTS

PREPARATION

5, 6, 7, 8	Close-lock, left leg back, arms second [228]
1	Rib cage left, hips right, left side forward [229]
2, 3	Left arm fifth, shoulders down [230]
4	Shoulders square, shift rib cage more left [231]
5, 6	Body straightens, legs first [232]
7, 8	Back attitude left [233]
1, 2	Close-lock left leg back, left arm second [234 and 235]
3, 4, 5, 6	Round down, then up, arms second [236]
7, 8	Lengthen the back [237]

REPEAT 1 more time.

Second Port de Bras: Contraction

[238]

[239]

[240]

238. Brush the left leg second to the half-toe, press the palms on the hips, pull the hips back, and bend both knees.

239. Pull the stomach in and lift the body up, dropping the elbows to the waist and the palms in front of the shoulders.

240. Reach the arms up, and straighten the legs.

241. Press the left side forward and the left leg in back to close-lock position. Reach the arms out and down to second position. Keep the head and focus straight forward.

[241]

COUNTS

1, 2	Left half-toe in second, palms on hips, grand plié, hips pull back [238]
3, 4	Lift the back up, elbows down [239]
5	Straighten the back and legs, arms reach high [240]
6, 7, 8	Left side forward, close-lock left leg back; arms to second [241]

REPEAT 2 times altogether. Then repeat the first sixteen counts of this exercise one more time before continuing into the next part—the change of direction.

Second Port de Bras:
Change of Direction

[242]

242. Lift the body and step onto the left foot in second-position demi-plié, pressing the left shoulder and hip forward. Then change the weight and direction, step onto the right leg. The left side stays forward in effacé.

243. Press the right side forward, then turn in passé left left, pointing the foot. The stomach in lifts the back.

244. The right shoulder presses forward into a step across, rolling down and turning out. Close-lock fourth, and lift the weight up above the lower part of the body.

[244]

[243]

COUNTS

5	Left side forward, left step second
6	Change of direction, step right second [242]
7	Right shoulder forward, left leg turned-in passé [243]
8	Close-lock left front, hips square, right shoulder forward [244]

REPEAT entire second port de bras on the other side (64 counts).

TURN OUT, TURN IN,
ATTITUDE, DOWN

The Turn Out, Turn In, Attitude, Down exercise helps you to find the balance going from the floor to passés, out or in. It teaches that, by using the buttocks, you control the turn-out position and the balancing on one leg. Also, the turning-in position gives you better flexibility to turn out. The hips become strong and flexible in both directions.

Whenever you need help balancing in any position, use the space around you. Your space is your barre.

[245]

[246]

[247]

[248]

[249]

245. Demi-plié both legs, and touch the right toes on the floor in an open front croisé position. Press the arms open to second position on an imaginary barre.

246. Straighten the left leg, and press the right leg to turn-out passé.

247. Turn in, passé right, trying not to twist the hips by keeping the knee low.

248. Turn out; passé right.

249. Demi-plié and tendu again.

250. Bend and swing the right leg open to second position; point the right foot, straighten the left leg, stretch open the thighs (side attitude).

251. Demi-plié, and touch the right toes on the floor again.

[250]

[251]

COUNTS

PREPARATION

5, 6, 7, 8	Balance on left, demi-plié, right touch open croisé, arms in second [245]
1, 2	Straighten left leg, right passé turned out [246]
3, 4	Right passé turned in [247]
5, 6	Right passé turned out [248]
7, 8	Demi-plié left, right touch open croisé [249]
1, 2	Second attitude right [250]
3, 4	Touch down, plié croisé [251]
5, 6	Second attitude right [250]
7, 8	Down [251]

REPEAT 3 more times.

REPEAT on the other side.

THIRD PORT DE BRAS:
Attitude Promenade

The Third Port de Bras starts with the Attitude Promenade. The attitude exercise came from my study of ballet and was especially important for me because I had trouble balancing while turning, due to my double vision. I put in this exercise to work on pivoting, to find balance and control while going in a circling movement. In dancing, this is one of the most difficult lessons of all to learn: how to pivot while standing on one leg. This exercise comes at this point in the technique because the body is by now prepared to attempt it.

Begin the attitude balance, and continue into stretches that use the body bending and balancing from one side to the other. Feel the flow of the body. Then finish with a final relevé where you balance as high on the toes as you can, feeling like you could go up and out forever.

252. Balance on the left leg, pulling the stomach in and shoulders down. Point the right foot; the arms press to first.

253. Turn out passé right and press the arms up forward of the hips, with the shoulders down.

[254]

[253]

[252]

[255]

[256]

254. Open the right thigh to a back attitude. Press the left arm down on the imaginary barre and the right arm to fifth, with curved elbows. Keep the ribs under to open across the back.

255. Lengthen the body and lift up the left heel to pivot left. Keep the shoulders down and the stomach in for control.

256. Continue to pivot left, circling with the elbows forward.

257. Pivot and circle back, opening the shoulders across the back.

258. Pivot to front to finish the circle (promenade).

259. Lift the arms to fifth with the shoulders down, and pull up off the left hip into passé, turn-out right.

260. Demi-plié the left leg; extend the right to front developpé. The arms press down in front of the chest, with the stomach pulling in.

261. Straighten the left leg, pull up off the left hip to circle point the right leg to second position.

262. Circle the right leg back and lengthen the muscles from the tailbone to the base of the skull.

[257]

[258]

[259]

[260]

[261]

[262]

COUNTS

PREPARATION

5, 6, 7, 8	Balance on left, right half-toe, arms first [252]
1, 2, 3, 4	Passé right, arms forward to fifth [253]
5, 6, 7, 8	Point back to attitude, right arm fifth, left second [254]
1–8	Heel lifts up to pivot full circle, lengthen back [255-258]
1, 2, 3, 4	Passé right, arms fifth [259]
5, 6, 7, 8	Plié left, point right front, arms front [260]
1, 2, 3, 4	Open right leg second, left straight [261]
5, 6, 7, 8	Right leg back; your space is the barre [262]

[263]

[264]

[265]

263. Slide the right foot through first position to fourth. Bend the right leg to half-toe. Reach both arms up through the back to fifth position, and press the right shoulder forward.

264. Drop the right heel, and straighten the leg for the hips to square front. Reach the left arm and left side forward, with the shoulders pulling down and the elbows curving.

265. Round the body down, with the arms in fifth.

266. Lift the back with the stomach in and the ribs under. Press the arms to second position.

267. Lift the weight up to open right passé.

268. Demi-plié right fourth position, keeping the back lifted.

[266]

[267]

[268]

COUNTS

1, 2, 3, 4	Brush right forward to half-toe, arms fifth, stretch right side [263]
5, 6, 7, 8	Heel turns in and down, legs straight, stretch left side, [264]
1, 2, 3, 4	Cross arms front, back rounds down [265]
5	Lift up, plié right, arms second [266]
6, 7	Passé right [267]
8	Demi-plié fourth [268]

REPEAT 3 more times and hold the last 6, 7, 8 count in passé.

269. Pivot the left heel back to turn the body to the diagonal, as the arms press forward.

270. Stretch the right leg back in arabesque, and pull back on the right shoulder to square to croisé. Stretch the arms open in second and try not to pinch the shoulders.

271. Press the body forward and down (panché). Use the stomach, shoulder, and buttock muscles to control. Stretch-point the right leg higher.

272. Lift the body to center and the leg will lower. Reach forward and adjust the balance.

273. Press down on the shoulders and armpits as if using a barre, and lift the back of the neck. Pull the stomach up into the chest; slowly roll up to relevé.

[269]

[270]

[271]

[272]

[273]

COUNTS

1, 2, 3, 4	Pivot left leg back, passé right, arms front [269]
5, 6, 7, 8	Right back arabesque, arms in second [270]
1-8	Straight back forward, lift leg [271]
1, 2, 3, 4	Lift the back [272]
5, 6, 7, 8	Slow relevé; your space is your barre [273]

FLOOR WORK

The next exercises are a series of floor exercises. They are very simple exercises because I believe floor work, as is done in modern dance, will strengthen the body and get through to muscles—to stretch and strengthen them—in a way you don't normally get from standing exercises. But I strongly believe that the body should be warmed up before sitting on the floor and stretching.

When sitting on the floor, make sure the body is lifted; pull the shoulders down and the stomach into the back. It's important to pull up on the thighs while stretching, to prevent straining the knees and over-stretching the legs.

The body should never be forced; everything should be very natural-looking. The more natural-looking, the more beautiful it is.

Circle the Insteps

Circling the insteps is for flexibility and strength of the ankles. It also builds up strength in the instep, arch, and point.

274. Sit with the legs straight out in front of the body, and lift the back up. Pull up on the thighs, and lift the right leg pointed low off the floor.

275. Flex the right foot up.

276. Stretch the right foot to the right, and circle out away from the left leg.

277. Continue the circle down, pointing the right foot straight again.

278. Flex the right foot in toward the left leg. Then complete the circle, flexing the foot up.

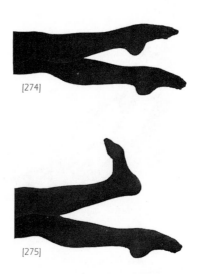

[274]

[275]

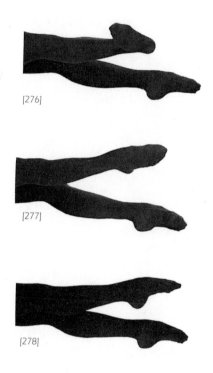

[276]

[277]

[278]

COUNTS

PREPARATION

5, 6, 7, 8	Lift right leg and point [274]
AND	Flex right foot up
1, 2	Complete circle to outside [275, 276, 277, 278]
3, 4	Repeat
5, 6	Repeat
7, 8	Repeat

REPEAT the circling outside, 1 more eight-count.

REVERSE the circling inside, 2 eights (8 circles) altogether.

REPEAT the same circling, outside then inside, with the left leg.

Forward and Back

This exercise develops the stomach muscles, to give you the strength to hold up your back. It also teaches you to pull up the muscles in the thighs, strengthening the muscles around the knees.

[279]

[280]

279. Pull the stomach in and the shoulders down; sit up over the tailbone. Press the arms to second position and point through the feet.

280. Keep the back straight, and press the body forward. Continue to lift up and out through the base of the skull.

281. Lift the body to center, and press the right shoulder forward to strengthen the épaulement. Pull the shoulders down as the arms press to first. Keep the focus front.

282. Return the shoulders square and the arms to second.

283. Press the body forward again, lengthening the spine.

284. Lift the body to center and press the left shoulder forward, with the arms in first position.

285. Square the shoulders, and open the arms to second again.

[281]

[282]

[283]

[284]

[285]

[286]

[287]

[288]

286. Reach the arms forward; round the back, pulling the stomach in.

287. Press the chin toward the chest, and round the back more. Circle the arms to second, then back of the hips.

288. Circle the arms in, and completely relax the back.

289. Lift the body up, pressing the arms forward.

290. Sit up; press the arms to second position.

COUNTS

PREPARATION

AND	Sit up, arms second, pointed feet [279]
1, 2	Body forward, return center [280]
3	Right épaulement forward, arms first [281]
4	Center, arms second [282]
5, 6	Body forward, return center [283]
7, 8	Left side forward, arms first [284]
8	Return center, arms second [285]

Reach and circle:

1	Round the spine, arms forward [286]
2	Head down, arms second, then back [287]
3, 4	Relax the spine, arms circle in to reach front [288]
5, 6	Lift the body, reach forward [289]
7, 8	Center, arms second [290]

REPEAT 3 more times (64 counts).

[289]

[290]

Développé

This exercise gives you strength in the leg and buttock muscles to extend the legs correctly—while strengthening the stomach.

291. Shift the weight back, bringing the elbows down and the palms down on the floor. Lengthen the spine and point through both feet.

292. Lift to bend the right leg to turned-in passé, and pull the stomach in to press the small of the back into the floor.

293. Développé; stretch-point the right leg up.

294. Return the right leg to a turned-in passé.

295. Développé the right leg up again.

296. Turn the right leg out from the hip, and slowly lower the straight leg to the floor.

[293]

[292]

[291]

[296]

[295]

[294]

COUNTS

PREPARATION

7, 8	Shift to elbows for last 7, 8 of previous exercise [291]
1, 2	Right leg turned-in passé, stretch spine [292]
3, 4	Développé up [293]
5	Turn in passé [294]
6	Développé up [295]
7, 8	Turn out leg from hip and lower down [296]

297. Extend both legs straight out on the floor.

298. Lift to bend both knees up, pressing them together as the small of the back presses into the floor. Pull the stomach in and the shoulders down.

299. Développé the legs straight up above the body. Try to keep the small of the back pressing into the floor.

300. Bend both knees again.

301. Repeat the développé; flex the feet and turn out from hips.

302. Use the stomach pulling in and the shoulders pulling down to stretch up through the heels and lower the legs.

303. Cross the right leg over the left.

[300]

[299]

[298]

[297]

[301]

[302]

[303]

COUNTS

AND	Lengthen both legs and stretch-point feet [297]
1, 2, 3, 4	Bend both legs, back into the floor [298]
5, 6, 7, 8	Développé up, shoulders down [299]
1, 2	Bend both legs [300]
3, 4	Développé [301]
5	Turn out from hips [301]
6, 7, 8	Straight legs down [302]

REPEAT 2 more times. On last 7,8, cross right leg over left [303].

304. Battement, kicking the right leg up. Pull the stomach in, with the shoulders down, and press the small of the back into the floor.

305. Keep the leg lifted, and flex the right foot, pressing up through the heel.

306. Stretch-point the right foot.

307. Lower the straight right leg down to cross over the left, using the stomach muscles to hold the small of the back into the floor.

308. Right battement straight up again, then lower right leg over left.

[305]

[304]

[308]

[307]

[306]

COUNTS

1, 2	Battement right [304]
3	Flex foot [305]
4	Stretch-point [306]
5	Leg down [307]
6, 7	Leg up and down [308]
8	Change left over right and REVERSE

REPEAT battement with left leg.

REPEAT 1 more time (32 counts).

135

309. Stretch-point through the feet with both legs down. Pull the shoulders so the back and neck are not pinching.

310. Pull the stomach in to press the small of the back into the floor. Be careful to keep the back from arching, and lift both legs straight up.

311. Turn out both legs from the hip and flex the heels.

312. Lengthen the spine; press forward through the heels. Lower the straight legs, making sure the back is held strong by pulling the stomach in.

[309]

[310]

[311]

[312]

313. (Side view) Lift the back and sit up. Press-point through the feet with the arms in front; the stomach is in and the shoulders down.

[313]

COUNTS

1, 2	Both legs straight, pointing [309]
3–8	Slowly lift legs up, stomach in [310]
1, 2	Lower legs to floor, feet flexed, stomach in [311]
3–7	Lift both legs straight up, stomach in [310]
8	Turn out from the hips and lower [311]

REPEAT 1 more time. Last 8 counts as follows:

1, 2, 3, 4	Lower half-way down, stomach in [312]
5, 6, 7, 8	Sit up, then lower the legs [313]

137

Relax the Back

This exercise stretches the muscles in the back, lengthens the spine, and develops the turn-out from the pelvis. It is repeated next with the legs in second position, but be sure to pull up on the thighs to protect the back of the legs from over-stretching.

[314]

[315]

314. Lengthen the back; sit up with the thighs open, the bottoms of the feet together and the heels lifted off the floor.

315. Pull the stomach in, pull the chin toward the chest, and round the shoulders to expand the muscles across the back.

316. Press the body forward and relax the back as the elbows bend. Drop the heels onto the floor.

317. Straighten the back, with the weight forward of the tailbone and the shoulders down.

318. Sit up over the tailbone and lengthen the back. Lift the heels again.

[316]

[317]

[318]

Relax the Back—Second Position

[319]

[320]

319. Straighten and open the legs to second position, with the legs turned out and pointing. Sit up over the tailbone, and lengthen the body, with the arms in second.

320. (Side view) Pull the stomach in, feeling the ribs pull under the chest, and shift the weight in back of the tailbone. The arms reach front, with the shoulders pulling down, as the back rounds, with the chin pressing toward the chest.

321. With the arms reaching forward, press the body forward and relax the back. It's important to keep the legs and feet turned out from the hips without rolling them forward.

322. Straighten the back and lengthen into the base of the skull.

323. Sit up over the tailbone, with the arms in second.

[321]

[322]

[323]

324.   Without sliding the heel, flex the right leg by bending the knee and foot up.

325.   Stretch-point the right leg to a full extension.

326–327.   Reverse on the left leg. Then flex both legs and extend.

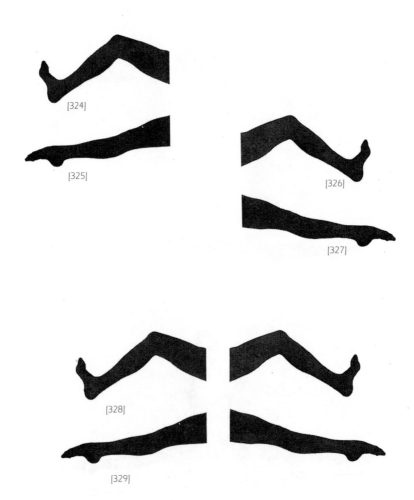

[324]

[325]

[326]

[327]

[328]

[329]

COUNTS

5, 6, 7, 8	Bottoms of feet together, knees bent, sit up, hold ankles [314]
1, 2, 3, 4	Stomach in, round shoulders, open across back [315]
5, 6, 7, 8	Relax, back forward, elbows bent [316]
1, 2, 3, 4	Straighten the back forward [317]
5, 6, 7, 8	Sit up [318]

REPEAT 3 more times.

1, 3, 5, 7	Press the thighs more open and down [314]
2, 4, 6, 8	Release [318]

REPEAT 6 times altogether (48 counts).

Relax Back Second:

PREPARATION

5, 6, 7, 8	Legs and arms in second, lengthen spine [319]
1, 2, 3, 4	Round the back [320]
5, 6, 7, 8	Relax forward, turned out from hip [321]
1, 2, 3, 4	Straighten the spine, stomach in [322]
5, 6, 7, 8	Sit up [323]

REPEAT 3 more times.

Flex Leg:

AND	Flex right, lift knee, left leg straight [324]
1, 3, 5, 7	Point right, knee down [325]
2, 4, 6, 8	Flex right, lift knee [324]
AND	Flex left leg, right leg straight
1, 3, 5, 7	Point left [326]
2, 4, 6, 8	Flex left [327]

CONTINUE with both legs flexing [328, 329].

Turn Down

The turn-down exercise is the same as the standing turn-down exercise in the pre-warm up. Use the stomach muscles in to hold up the back, and the thighs pulling up to protect the legs.

[330]

[331]

[332]

[333]

[334]

330. Sit up over the tailbone; lengthen the spine, with the arms in second position.

331. Turn the body left to the diagonal, with the body lifted.

332. Pull the stomach in, press the body forward slightly toward the floor while keeping the back straight. This is not a rounded back with the head and shoulders rounded, but a straight-back stretch of the muscles in the small of the back. Keep the body, inside both legs—not twisted over the left leg.

333. Lift the body up.

334. Turn center, squaring the shoulders front.

335. Turn the body right to the diagonal.

336. Press the straight back forward, toward the floor, with the elbows lifted and curved in second position.

337. Lift the back up, with the stomach in.

338. Return to center.

[335]

[336]

[337]

[338]

339. Press the body forward toward the floor while the arms stay open across the back and the legs turn out.

340. Lift the body to sit up, and press the right shoulder forward; the arms press to first position.

341. Repeat; with a straight back, press the body forward, with the arms in second.

342. Sit up and press the left shoulder forward; arms in first.

[339]

[340]

[341]

[342]

343. Turn the body to the left diagonal again, with the arms in second.

344. Round the spine, pressing the chin against the chest and the forehead toward the floor, inside the left leg. The arms relax on each side of the left leg.

345. Side-stretch right, with the right arm circling outside through first position to fifth; the left arm moves into fifth position.

[343]

[344]

[345]

346. Reach the body forward; the torso and arms swing front. Keep the legs turned out from the hips.

347. Half-circle into a side-stretch left, reaching over the right leg, keeping both the hips and buttocks pressed down into the floor.

348. Lift the body up to center, with the left arm in fifth position; then both arms press to second.

[346]

[347]

[348]

[349]

[350]

[351]

[352]

349. Bring the legs together and round the spine; reach the arms over the feet.

350. Pull the stomach in to lift the back, and bend both knees.

351. Lengthen the spine and kick, pointing straight out, with the legs together. Reach the arms up and then forward.

352. Land the legs and body comfortably down, and relax the body over the legs.

COUNTS

PREPARATION

5, 6, 7, 8	Lift the back, stomach in, arms second [330]
1, 2	Turn left diagonal [331]
3, 4	Body presses forward [332]
5, 6	Lift body up [333]
7, 8	Center [334]
1, 2	Turn diagonal right [335]
3, 4	Body presses forward [336]
5, 6	Lift up [337]
7, 8	Center [338]
1, 2	Straight back forward [339]
3, 4	Lift up, right shoulder forward [340]
5, 6	Straight forward, no roll-in of legs [341]
7, 8	Lift up, left shoulder forward [342]

REPEAT 8 count with straight back forward 1 more time.
REPEAT turn down right, left, front 1 more time

Turn Down, Side-Stretch:

1–8	Turn left, round the back, hands on sides of legs [343, 344]
1, 2, 3, 4	Side-stretch right, shoulders down [335]
5	Swing forward, arms fifth [346]
6	Half-circle, side-stretch left [347]
7, 8	Arms fifth to second, sit up [348]

REPEAT to right side.
REPEAT right and left turn, then down, and side-stretch 3 more times.

7, 8 AND	Legs together
1	Round the back, reach arms over toes [349]
2, 3	Stomach in, sit up, knees bend, arms in [350]
4	Lift the back, straighten legs, point and turn out [351]

REPEAT 7 more times (28 counts).
FINISH last 4 counts, holding the legs up [352].

Kickout on Stomach, Side, Back

This exercise develops the muscles in the pelvis so that you are not arching the back when standing. Press the hip muscles down into the floor without lifting them or arching the back. Make sure to pull the shoulders down and to lengthen into the base of the skull.

[353]

[354]

[355]

[356]

[357]

353. Roll over onto the stomach. Straighten the legs comfortably on the floor with the hips down, and lift the back up. The palms and elbows press down to support the spine.

354. Stretch right leg straight back and up, with the hips down.

355. Lower the right leg to the floor.

356. Stretch the left leg up.

357. Lower the left leg.

358. Roll over onto the left side, and lift the chest up by resting the left forearm. Stretch the right arm to second and lengthen the neck. Bend the left leg to turn-in passé and the right leg to turn-out passé, behind the right arm.

359. Développé the right leg behind the right shoulder.

360. Repeat to turn-out passé.

[358]

[359]

[360]

361. Lie flat on the back and lengthen the spine, pressing the small of the back down.

362. Bend the right knee up, and grab hold of the leg, pressing the small of the back more into the floor. Keep the hips and shoulders down.

363. The arms hold the back of the calf and ankle to straighten the right leg comfortably. Point through both feet.

364. Bend the right knee, and stretch the back of the thigh and buttocks, with the arms pulling the knee close.

365. Release the right leg down, and relax.

[361]

[362]

[363]

[364]

[365]

COUNTS

5, 6, 7, 8	Roll on stomach, rest on forearms, legs straight [353]
1	Hips on floor, lift-point the right leg [354]
2	Release right leg down [355]
3	Left leg up [356]
4	Left leg down [357]

REPEAT alternating right and left leg 1 more 8-count; then roll onto left hip and forearm, chest up; bend both knees [358]

1	Straighten right leg, right arm in second [359]
2	Bend the right knee [360]
3	Point up [361]
4	Bend [362]

REPEAT right kick 2 eights altogether.

REPEAT on the other side.

AND	Roll onto the back, legs straight pointing {363}
1, 2, 3, 4	Bend right knee toward right shoulder [364]
5, 6, 7, 8	Straighten leg, hands hold calf, shoulders down [365]
1, 2, 3, 4	Bend right knee, stretching with hands [366]
5, 6, 7, 8	Relax leg down [367]

Stretch left leg 2 eights.

REPEAT right, then left, 4 times altogether (64 counts) to finish.

LAST STRETCH

The last stretch is a synopsis of all the exercises. It's a slight review of everything that went before—bending forward, bending back, bending side, and rounding movements—all of the directions that the body can go in so that the spine is completely lengthened and safely prepared to dance, or do anything.

It starts with the head stretching back, then front, then side to side, then half-circles into full circles, with the shoulders pressing down and level. By releasing the tension in the neck and shoulders, you can help the whole body's circulation and strengthen your voice and eyesight. It will also help to focus turns in dance (spotting) by relaxing the neck muscles.

The middle and end of this exercise stretches in every direction to make sure that the body is completely warmed up. I believe in rounding forward before doing any backbends, so that you lengthen the spine and strengthen the muscles around the vertebrae. I feel that, when warming up, a backbend should be at your own pace.

The warmer the body, the greater the elasticity. Strength comes from elasticity, not tension.

Circle the Head

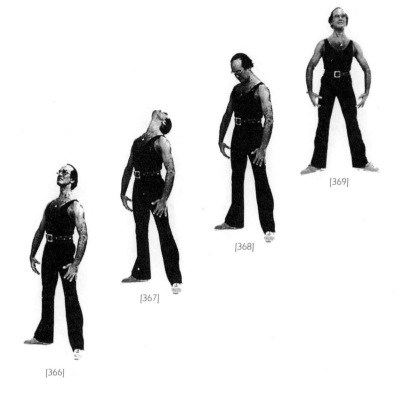

[369]

[368]

[367]

[366]

366. To prepare, stand with the legs in second position, the stomach in, the shoulders down. Squeeze the buttocks to pull up on the thighs, and lengthen the spine into the base of the skull and beyond.

367. Lift the chin, and control the head going back comfortably. Feel the stretch in the neck and chest muscles.

368. Press the chin comfortably toward the chest. Feel the stretch in back of the neck and across the shoulders.

369. Return to center.

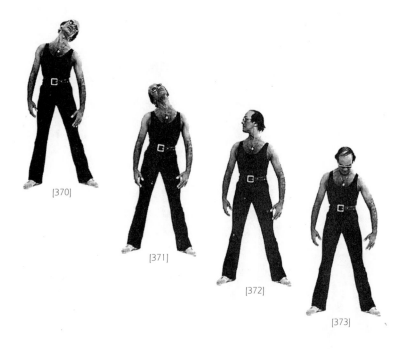

[370]

[371]

[372]

[373]

370. Keep the shoulders level, and tilt the head to the left. Feel the muscles stretch from the face into the right fingertips.

371. Lift the head to center, then tilt the head right. Feel the stretch into the left fingertips.

372. Return to center, then turn the head to the right and focus the eyes at eye level.

373. Roll the head down comfortably.

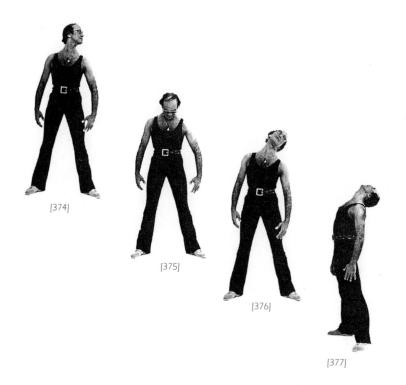

[374]

[375]

[376]

[377]

374. Half-circle the head to the left side, and focus your eyes to the left side of the room.

375. Press the chin toward the chest to start a full head circle to the left.

376. Circle the head to the left side.

377. (Side view) Continue circling back, trying not to pinch the shoulders back. Then to the right side and down to center, to complete a full circle.

COUNTS

PREPARATION

5, 6, 7, 8   Stand second, shoulders down, stomach in, buttocks tighten [366]

1, 2   Head back [367]

3   Head forward [368]

4   Center [369]

REPEAT 2 eights altogether.

1, 2   Shoulders down and level, tilt head left [370]

3, 4   Pass center, tilt head right, center [371]

REPEAT 2 eights altogether.

1, 2   Turn head right [372]

3–8   Half-circle down to left [373–374]

1–8   Half circle down to right [374–373].

REPEAT right and left 1 more time.

1, 2, 3, 4   Head down [375]

5, 6, 7, 8   Head left [376]

1, 2, 3, 4   Head back [377]

5, 6, 7, 8   Head right [378]

REPEAT full circle left 1 more time.

Turn Down

[379]

[378]

378. Standing in second, turn the body to the left diagonal, lifting the right heel up and right arm to fifth. Pull the shoulders down, and square the body to the diagonal without over-rotating the back to the left.

379. With the right arm leading down, round the back, relaxing the head, with the heel down.

[380]

[381]

[382]

[383]

380. Pivot the right heel to second position; turn the torso center.

381. Pivot the left heel out; switch the left arm to lead the circle up.

382. Lift the body and the left heel up.

383. Pivot the left heel to second position; turn the hips and shoulders center; bring the right arm to fifth position.

384. Repeat the circle, turning the body to the right diagonal.

385. Pivot the right heel out; turn the torso left, lead with the right arm.

386. Circle up, with the right arm and heel lifted. Then complete the circle; pivot to second; turn the hips and shoulders front.

[384]

[385]

[386]

COUNTS

1, 2	Turn, left heel up, right arm fifth, left second [378]
3, 4, 5, 6	Round the spine, left heel down [379]
7, 8	Pivot second, both arms down [380]
1, 2, 3, 4	Switch arms [381]
5, 6	Complete circle up, left heel up, left arm fifth, right arm second [382]
7, 8	Turn center into second position, arms in fifth [383]

REPEAT to the right, full circle [384–386].

REPEAT. Left and right full circles 3 more times.

Pliés in Second

[387]

[388]

[389]

[390]

387. Pull the stomach in, the shoulders down, and pull up on the thighs.

388. Keep the feet firmly on the ground, the knees over the toes, and grand plié. The arms press down through first position.

389. Lift the back to straighten the legs; the arms press to second.

390. Grand plié again in second position, as the arms press to first.

391. Then press the arms to fifth position, keeping the shoulders down as the legs straighten.

392. Pull the stomach into the back, and press the hips back. Reach the arms forward, and pull up on the thigh muscles.

393. Lift the body straight up, pull the shoulders and armpits down, and tighten the buttocks.

[393]

[392]

[391]

394. Grand plié again in second; the arms press to first.

395. Straighten the legs, and press the arms to second.

396. Repeat grand plié in second, keeping the knees over the toes and the hips forward. Press the arms down through first.

397. Pull the stomach in to lift the weight and straighten the legs, while the arms raise to fifth. Press the shoulders down, lengthen the spine, tighten the buttocks, and relevé.

[394]

[395]

[396]

[397]

398. Grand plié in second, and press the arms to first.

399. Shift the body to side-stretch right, and press the left arm to second as the right arm swings across the chest.

400. Feel the full side-stretch right with the legs straightening and the right arm in fifth. Pull the shoulders down.

401. Plié in second, shifting the body to center; the right arm swings down through first.

402. Pull up to center; straighten the legs; press the arms second.

[398]

[399]

[400]

[401]

[402]

403. Grand plié in second, and press the arms to first.

404. Side-stretch left, and swing the left arm across the chest.

405. Complete the side-stretch.

406. Plié in second again, shifting the weight to center.

407. Straighten the body center, and press the arms to second.

[403]

[404]

[405]

[406]

[407]

COUNTS

1, 2	Plié second, arms first [388]
3, 4	Legs straighten, arms second [389]
5, 6	Plié second, arms down [390]
7, 8	Legs straighten, arms fifth, shoulders down [391]
1, 2, 3, 4	Hips back, back straight, stomach in [392]
5, 6, 7, 8	Lift the body [393]
1, 2	Plié second, arms down [394]
3, 4	Legs straighten, arms second [395]
5, 6	Plié second, arms down [396]
7, 8	Legs straighten, arms fifth, relevé [397]

Plié side-stretch:

1, 2	Plié second, arms down [398]
3	Right side-stretch [399]
4	Legs straighten, shoulders down [400]
5, 6	Plié second, right arm down [401]
7, 8	Legs straighten, arms second [402]
1–8	Plié, side-stretch left [403–407]

REPEAT right and left side-stretches 1 more time.

Backbend

When doing a backbend, place the legs comfortably apart, the toes forward, and the weight equal on both feet, solid to the ground. The most important thing to do is tighten the buttocks and press the pelvis forward. Then, lift up the chest, look back, and after you are as far as you can go, bend the knees last. (The word is "backbend," not bend-back.) Make sure you are not rolling in on the knees or feet. Lift off the back and then straighten the body.

Don't do a backbend if you have a bad back.

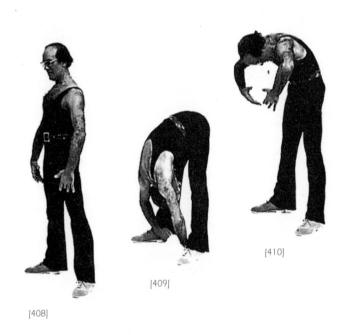

[408]

[409]

[410]

408. Adjust the legs in to a closer second position, with the knees over the toes. Press the chin toward the chest to start the roll-down.

409. Round the back from the tailbone to the base of the skull, dropping the arms down, with a slight plié.

410. Suck in the stomach to align the vertebrae and roll up. Press the elbows out with the palms toward the chest.

[411]

[412]

[413]

411. Straighten the body and tighten the buttocks, pressing the pelvis forward. Lift the chest up. Reach forward through the fingertips.

412. Lift the chest high off the back and look back.

413. Complete back-bend, tighten the buttocks, bend the knees over the toes, reach and resist forward.

414. Lift up out of the back, and slowly straighten the legs.

415. Lengthen up to center.

[414]

[415]

COUNTS

1, 2, 3, 4	Legs closer second, roll down [408–409]
5, 6, 7, 8	Roll up [410]
1	Hips forward, buttocks, tighten, chin down [411]
2, 3	Lift the back, look back, arms press forward [412]
4	Knees bend, press forward [413]
8	Center [415]

REPEAT 3 more times.

KICKOUTS

The last exercise is the kickout, or battement. I feel that when the body is completely warmed up, then it is ready to do the kicks. I do développé kicks, which are more jazzy.

The kick starts from close-lock fourth position into a développé, then returns back into close-lock. Feel, at the height of the extension, that the back and both legs are straight.

I believe that during the course of the exercises, in all of the warmups, the legs don't have to be very high off the ground. The height of the extension should be the height of the control of it. Using control of the body will give the kick an elongated look, a balanced look, and a much better stretch. Also, using the space as your barre will give more control to the kick. The kick should look completely controlled going up and down. The leg should look as though it were suspended in the air.

The beauty of a kick is the control of the whole body.

Kickouts, Front

[416]

[417]

[418]

416. Press the right leg behind the left in close-lock fourth position. Press the arms to second position.

417. Lift the back as the right leg lifts and bends to a turned-in passé.

418. Développé, kicking the right leg forward, and straighten the supporting left leg. Keep the back straight and lifting, with the shoulders down as the leg extends.

419. Bring the right leg back to turned-in passé.

420. Return the right leg behind the left to close-lock fourth.

[419]

[420]

COUNTS

PREPARATION

5, 6, 7, 8	Close-lock right leg back, arms second [416]
1	Turned-in passé right [417]
2	Développé right leg; straighten left [418]
3	Turned-in passé right [419]
4	Close-lock right leg back [420]

REPEAT 7 more times.

There is an eight-count break to switch legs.

REPEAT front kicks with left leg 8 times altogether.

Kickouts, Side

[421]

[422]

[423]

[424]

421. Press the right leg in back of the left, in close-lock position.

422. Lift the right leg to turn out in passé, pointing the right foot.

423. Développé, kicking à la second (second), straightening both knees, with the leg behind the arms in second.

424. Bend the right knee in, to turned-out passé.

[428]

[427]

[426]

[425]

425. Return the right leg behind the left to close-lock position.

426. Lift the right leg to turned-out passé, and press the left shoulder forward. Keep the arms in second and the focus front.

427. Développé and point second, straightening both legs. Lift the back and press the shoulders down for more control.

428. Lengthen the spine and land the right leg in second plié.

Kickouts, Back

[429]

[430]

[431]

429. Center the balance, with the legs meeting in first position and the arms open in second.

430. Demi-plié the left leg, and point the right leg front, turning the heel forward.

431. Brush the right leg back to first position.

432. Continue brushing the right leg straight back to arabesque, lifting it comfortably off the floor. Use the stomach muscles, pulling in to lift up, not arch, the back.

433. Bring the right leg forward to passé.

434. Demi-plié the left leg, and point the right leg front, turning the heel forward.

WITHDRAWN

COUNTS

PREPARATION

5, 6	Center, feet in first, arms second [429]
7, 8	Point right front, demi-plié left
1, 2	Brush-point back, arabesque [431–432]
3	Right turn out passé, demi-plié left [433]
4	Point right front [434]

REPEAT 7 more times.

REPEAT with left leg 8 times.

[432]

[433]

[434]

179

"This is the end of my exercises.
I hope they help you as much as
they help me. Thank you, and
Never Stop Moving!!"

THE CO-AUTHORS

Lorraine Person Kriegel has a Master's Degree in Dance Aesthetics from UCLA. She worked as a choreographer, dancer, and artistic director for twenty years throughout Europe and the Americas. In 1985, she choreographed a national tour of jazz music's legendary performers.

Lorraine has studied with Luigi since 1970, but it was when teaching jazz dance history at UCLA and the University of Calgary that she developed a theoretical understanding and respect for the Luigi technique as a language of jazz. She now teaches Luigi's technique in Europe and New York. Her previous book, co authored with Kim Chandler-Vaccaro, is a college text, "Jazz Dance Today."

Francis J. Roach was first a student and now a protegé of dance legend Luigi. He travels the world teaching, performing, and choreographing this "classical jazz" technique far from his hometown of Conneaut, Ohio. Francis has danced on Broadway and TV specials, in films and stock companies, guested with dance companies, and starred in his own concert tour of Japan. His choreography jobs include industrials, commercials, MTV videos, off-Broadway, and stock musicals. He has been on faculty, teaching Luigi technique at many colleges, universities, and dance tours. Francis is proudest of passing on Luigi's sophisticated, elegant, and innovative technique which teaches everyone to truly "feel from the inside" and to "listen to the sound of your soul and dance with it."